It’s one thing to teach the truth, a ... ot
only interpreting Scripture but fi ... er-
preted by it. That is what happens ... ets
the preacher and hears Christ. Joh ... he
Christian life is simply growth in seeing ... ing
these sermons, I found myself joining in his joyful “Amen!” to all of the promises that we have in Jesus Christ. What could be more rewarding than that?”

Michael Horton

Prof. of Theology and Apologetics, Westminster Seminary California
Author, *The Christian Faith* (Zondervan)

I used *The Grace of Truth* for daily devotions and it was superb. Stimulating and refreshing, it takes the reader to the truth about God and about our human condition. Pastoral, cliché-free and accessible, John Webster’s book will be returned to often. I commend it strongly.

Dominic Smart

Minister, Gilcomston South Church, Aberdeen, Scotland
Visiting Lecturer, Highland Theological College, Scotland
Author, *When We Get it Wrong* (Authentic)

John Webster displays a great sense of the power of the English language and an even greater sense of the reliability of Holy Scripture and the power of the gospel. Together these make compelling and inspiring reading.

Graeme Goldsworthy

Visiting Lecturer in Hermeneutics, Moore College, Australia
Author, *Preaching the Whole Bible as Christian Scripture* (Eerdmans)

Splendid sermons, and not just as models for aspiring preachers! Unobtrusive scholarship, meticulous listening to Scripture and close observation of the human predicament combine to give us God’s word just where we need it.

Donald Macleod

Prof. of Systematic Theology, Free Church of Scotland College
Author, *A Faith to Live By* (Mentor)

These are sermons of a high order, carefully and constantly attentive to the Biblical text, and alive to the deep realities of human life. The attentive reader will both learn and grow.

Stephen Holmes

Senior Lecturer in Theology, University of St. Andrews, Scotland
Author, *The Wondrous Cross* (Paternoster)

John Webster's work is beautifully written, unfailingly encouraging, and thoroughly Christ-centered. It is pure gospel—aged and distilled out of years of theological reflection and biblical study. Here indeed is a work that lifts our eyes to the heavens, from whence our help still comes.

Noel Due

Honorary Teaching Fellow, Highland Theological College, Scotland
Visiting Lecturer, Adelaide College of Ministries, Australia
Author, *Created for Worship* (Christian Focus)

This superb book provides an invaluable opportunity to engage with the preaching of one of the world's leading contemporary evangelical theologians. This should prove of immense interest to lay people, clergy, students and academics alike.

Alan Torrance

Prof. of Systematic Theology, University of St. Andrews, Scotland
Author, *Persons in Communion* (T&T Clark)

These collected sermons from Professor John Webster are rich in biblical content, perceptive in their diagnosis of the human condition, Christ-centered in their focus, and filled with hope through the gospel. Read and savor these sermons that you might repent, believe, and persevere to the glory of Christ!

Steven Roy

Assoc. Prof. of Pastoral Theology, Trinity Evangelical Divinity School
Author, *What God Thinks When We Fail* (InterVarsity)

It has been said that if all our preachers were theologians and all our theologians were preachers, the Church would be in a much healthier condition. How good then to read these sermons from one of our leading British theologians, testimony to the fact that the only theology worth pursuing arises out of the life of the Church. John demonstrates that the complexity and depth of his understanding of the grace of God in Christ can be made not only accessible but challenging, stimulating and thrilling.

A.T.B. McGowan

Minister, Inverness East Church of Scotland
Prof. of Theology, University of the Highlands and Islands
Author, *The Divine Authenticity of Scripture* (InterVarsity)

CONFRONTED BY GRACE

CONFRONTED BY GRACE

Meditations of a Theologian

JOHN WEBSTER

Edited by Daniel Bush & Brannon Ellis

Confronted by Grace: Meditations of a Theologian

Edited by Daniel Bush & Brannon Ellis

Lexham Press, 1313 Commercial St., Bellingham, WA 98225
LexhamPress.com

Previously published as *The Grace of Truth* (Farmington Hills, Mich.: Oil Lamp Books LLC, 2011).

ISBN 978-1-57-799627-9

Lexham Editorial Team: David Bomar, Lynnea Fraser
Cover Design: Christine Gerhart
Typesetting: ProjectLuz.com

FOR MY BROTHER

MICHAEL WEBSTER

Contents

Preface

PREACHING IS ONE of the principal ways in which the God of the gospel has dealings with us. The gospel's God is eloquent: He does not remain locked in silence, but speaks. He does this supremely in the mission of the Son of God, the very Word of God who becomes flesh, communicating with human creatures in human ways, most of all in human speech. The Son of God comes as a preacher (Mark 1:38); this is a primary purpose and one of the most characteristic activities of his earthly ministry. His apostles, too, are summoned by him to preach the gospel: to speak from him and about him, to address their fellow creatures with testimony to the gospel. And this apostolic commission remains for the Church. Paul's charge to Timothy—"Preach the word" (2 Timothy 4:2)—extends to the Christian community now, and faithfulness to the charge is basic to the way in which the Church fulfills its nature and mission as the community of the Word of God. The Church of the Word is a Church in which, alongside praise, prayer, lament, sacraments, witness, service, fellowship and much else, there takes place the work of preaching.

There are at least three elements to preaching. First: Holy Scripture. Scripture is the body of texts which God forms to be his "Word," his communication with us in human language. In these texts, God teaches us, gives us knowledge—of himself, of ourselves, and of his ways with us. Preaching is not any sort of public Christian discourse; it is the Church saying something about the words of this text, on the basis of the words of this text, under this text's authority, direction and judgment. Second: the congregation. At the Lord's summons, the people of God gather in his presence. They gather in the expectation that something from God will be said to them—that however anxious, weary or indifferent they may be, the God of the gospel will address them with the gospel, will help them to hear what he says, and will instruct them on how to live life in his company. Third: the sermon. God speaks to the congregation through the human words of one who is appointed by God to "minister" the Word, to be an auxiliary in God's own speaking. The sermon repeats the scriptural Word in other human words, following the Word's movement and submitting to its rule. In this, the sermon assists in the work of the divine Word, which builds up the Church, making its life deep, steady, and vital.

The sermons in this book hardly match up to this understanding of preaching. Reading them through, I am acutely conscious that much could be said differently and better. Most of them were delivered in the years when I served as a canon of Christ Church cathedral in Oxford; a few were preached elsewhere. Daniel Bush and Brannon Ellis undertook the rather arduous task of editing the texts and preparing for publication, improving them a great deal in the process; I am grateful for their help.

John Webster
Aberdeen, Scotland

Part I

GRAVITY AND GRACE

CHAPTER 1

THE LIE OF SELF-SUFFICIENCY

Matthew 21:33–39

There was a master of a house who planted a vineyard and put a fence around it and dug a winepress in it and built a tower and leased it to tenants, and went into another country. When the season for fruit drew near, he sent his servants to the tenants to get his fruit. And the tenants took his servants and beat one, killed another, and stoned another. Again he sent other servants, more than the first. And they did the same to them. Finally he sent his son to them, saying, "They will respect my son." But when the tenants saw the son, they said to themselves, "This is the heir. Come, let us kill him and have his inheritance." And they took him and threw him out of the vineyard and killed him.

Matthew 21:33–39

One way of coming to understand the events of Holy Week is to think of them as the triumph of *falsehood*. Beginning on Palm Sunday with the story of Jesus' triumphal entry into Jerusalem and over the next few days moving inexorably to its climax, the drama of the passion unfolds as one thing: as a consistent, willful, institutionally orchestrated rejection of the truth—as the acting out of a lie.

What unites the cast of characters which are assembling before us as we read through the narratives of the passion of Christ is this: all together—religious leaders, the disciples, the governing authorities in the person of Pilate, and the chorus of minor players—in their various ways conspire to deny the truth. They all choose darkness rather than light; they all fail to acknowledge what above all they ought to acknowledge, that in the man Jesus they are faced with the presence of God himself. And the events in which they are caught up, the putting to death of the Son of God, are as a whole and in all their detail the embodiment of *the* great lie, the ultimate untruth.

Why do we tell lies? We lie to evade reality; we lie because the truth is too painful or too shameful for us to face, or because the truth is simply inconvenient and has to be suppressed before it's allowed to disturb us. We invent lies because, for whatever reason, we want to invent reality. And the false reality which we invent, the world we make up by our lying, has one great advantage for us: It makes no claims on us. It demands nothing. It doesn't shape us in the way that truth shapes us; it faces us with no obligations; it has no hard, resistant surfaces which we can't get through. A lie is a made-up reality, and so never unsettles, never criticizes, never resists, never overthrows us. It's the world, not as it is, but as we wish it to be: a world organized around us and our desires, the perfect environment in which we can be left at peace to be ourselves and to follow our own good or evil purposes.

Lies are a desperately destructive force in human life. When they take the form of private fantasy, they rob us of our ability to deal truthfully with the outside world; but when lies go public, when an entire social group replaces reality with untruth, then the consequences are deadly. Sometimes, indeed, they can be literally deadly: Lies can kill. Lies work only when they remain unexposed. Once truth is allowed out, once reality is let in, then the lie just vanishes; the whole world of falsehood just crashes to the ground. And if the lie is to be maintained intact, then anything which speaks the truth has to be got rid of.

Totalitarian societies, dishonest businesses, abusive human relationships—they all depend on the exclusion of truth and truth-speakers, making sure that what really is the case isn't allowed to come to light. Lies only work when they aren't shown up for what they are; and that's why lies always breed more lies, as we try to protect the world we've invented from being exposed.

At the heart of the story of the passion, therefore, is the confrontation of truth and falsehood. Why does Christ die? Why is he suppressed, cast out and finally silenced by death? Because he speaks the truth. He dies because in him there is spoken the truth of the human condition. He is the truth. In his person, as the one who he is, as the one who does what he does and says what he says, he announces the truth of the world, and thereby exposes its untruth. He shows up human falsehood in all its depravity. And he does so, not as a relatively truthful human person, nor even as a prophet inspired to declare what is hidden, but as God himself. His words, his declaration of the truth, are God's declaration. He is therefore truth in all its finality; truth unadorned, truth which interrupts and casts down every human lie, every obstacle to seeing reality as it is. In him there is a complete judgment, an unambiguous showing of the truth from which we may not hide. It's this which is at the core of the conflict between Jesus and Israel; and it's for this that he is sent to his death. What is the final terror which he evokes in those who hear him? Simply this: "they perceived that he was speaking about *them*."

Now, it is of this deadly struggle between truth and lies that we hear in Jesus' parable of the wicked husbandmen or the wicked tenants. Taking up a familiar picture from Isaiah of the chosen people as a vineyard planted by God, the parable condenses into a single story the whole drama of conflict which is unfolding before us in the last days of Jesus. The situation we are in, Jesus tells his contemporaries, is this: The people of God, God's chosen ones, are like a well set-up tenant farm, run by rogues who simply don't want to pay the rent. Indeed, not only do they refuse to pay, they even want to obliterate the whole idea that they are tenants and that they are responsible to the farm's owner. They want to go about their business as if there were no owner; and so when the owner sends his representatives, and even when he arrives in the person of his son, they act out the great lie they have built around themselves—they kill to get rid of any trace of the owner's demands, and so try to make a reality out of the falsehood that this is their farm which is owed to no one. Such, Jesus says, is Israel's situation; such is what is happening now in the life of the people of God. Truth, reality, the truth and reality of our situation as the people of God, are being overturned and replaced by a lie.

There are two things we must consider here if we are to let this story do its work among us. We must ask, first, about the nature of this final act of rebellion against God; and we must ask, second, about the identity of those who rebel in this way.

What is this act of refusal of God? At its heart, it's a refusal to consent to the reality of their situation as those who owe everything to God. Like tenants who pretend that what they rent is really their own property to do what they like with, so Israel lives by denying the reality of God. Above all, Israel denies that they are what they are because of God's *covenant*. God's covenant is God's utterly undeserved mercy, the abundant overflow of God's free grace in which God makes Israel out of nothing. As covenant people, they owe their life to God's giving, God's work, God's Word, God's promise. In truth, Israel lives, not out of their own resources, but out of grace. And it is exactly that which Israel now denies, Jesus tells them. Israel replaces this truth by the falsehood which says: We are not the creatures of grace; we are not the Lord's people; we are our own. This is our world, our society, our culture, our religion, ours to hold, ours to manage, ours to police, ours to possess at all costs. In effect, says Jesus, Israel is turning their back on their whole history, on the whole story of God's dealings with them from the exodus until now, undertaking the final folly of declaring independence from God.

When that happens—when independence is declared—then the first thing that goes out of the window is *obligation*. The first and most tenacious lie that has to be set up is that Israel owes nothing to God. Once grace is spurned, law is abolished. But maintaining that lie can be done only at a fearful price. The lie can be kept intact only if anything which threatens to expose it is destroyed. Anything which sets Israel's obligations before its eyes must be resisted and, in the end, obliterated—like the tenants who beat, and stone, and kill the householder's servants and then, finally, his very son.

The voice of obligation—the voice that intrudes into the self-satisfied and closed life of Israel and forces it to remember the covenant in which it is bound to God; the voice of the prophets, and ultimately of Jesus himself—must be silenced. As we listen over the next few days to the story of the passion, it is precisely this that we see: the increasing silence of Jesus as he is handed over to those who can survive intact only if they push him away and ultimately destroy him.

It's crucial, however, to grasp that this terrible falsehood presents itself as *religion*. The great wickedness of the events of the passion is not seen in the Gentiles who are caught up in the mess; it is seen in Israel. Israel's rejection of Jesus is in the name of religion. What is it that Israel found so ultimately offensive in Jesus? Not, in the end, his call for holiness, or his acts of power, or even his prophecy. All that in some shape or form could be absorbed into the lie which Israel had become. No, what really offended was his declaration that Israel's religious culture was itself a rebellion against God. What offended was his declaration that law was being reduced to performance. What offended was his denunciation of the whole cultural apparatus of holiness as a way of controlling God. Above all, what offended was his insistence that to be Israel they must listen, not to themselves, nor to their settled accounts of God, but to himself, to Jesus, as the one in and as whom God was now calling Israel to repentance. There is the offense—and therefore by oppression and judgment he was taken away.

Such is the refusal of God which we here witness. But who perpetrates it? Who are these wicked tenants who seek to possess what is not theirs? It's clear that they are Israel, and Israel personified most of all in the persons of its leaders, the chief priests and the Pharisees. But if we are to hear the witness of Scripture properly, we need to be especially careful and clear at this point. Israel acts in the name of and in the place of all.

This collection of assorted religious leaders is not just a particularly wicked set of specimens, whom we can inspect and then congratulate ourselves by saying we would have done otherwise. Not at all: They act in our name, they take our place. In doing what they do, in acting out the lie of self-sufficiency, in rebelling against the covenant of grace, they are merely doing what we do. Israel here is humanity itself in its hatred of God. The story of the passion is thus not just the central episode of Jewish history, but of all human history. Here is acted out our rejection of God, our covenant-breaking, our falsehood. And what therefore is condemned is *us*.

These are, of course, hard thoughts: There is an almost unrelieved bleakness to the parable which, if we really hear it, ought to shake us. But over this passage, and indeed over the whole dark story of the passion, there stands one great *Nevertheless*, one great word of the gospel which pronounces that—despite everything, despite the worst that human wickedness can do—God's covenant with humanity is undefeated.

That "Nevertheless" is declared to us in Psalm 80, which is one more variation on the theme of Israel as the vineyard planted by God. "You brought a vine out of Egypt; you drove out the nations and planted it" (80:8); but it was smashed, looted, broken down. Where is hope to be found? It is to be found in this prayer at the end of the psalm: "Restore us, O LORD God of hosts! Let your face shine, that we may be saved!" (80:19).

What is the only hope? That the face of God may shine upon us. That God may so present us with the truth that our falsehood is put away. That God may restore us by interposing himself between us and our destruction. That God will intercept our death-dealing ways and give us life.

It's the conviction of Christian faith that that prayer has already been answered, finally, fully and with absolute sufficiency, in the events of Good Friday and Easter Day. It's the conviction of Christian faith that Israel was not allowed to destroy itself or to reject its God. It's the conviction of Christian faith that human falsehood has been set aside once for all, that God's covenant stands, and that we stand within that covenant by his mercy alone. And that is why we may approach Holy Week with this prayer in our mouths:

> *Turn again, O God of hosts! Look down from heaven, and see. … Then we shall not turn back from you; give us life, and we will call upon your name! (Psalm 80:14, 18).*

CHAPTER 2

THE GREAT CONTRAST

Romans 5:12–21

Therefore, just as sin came into the world through one man, and death through sin, and so death spread to all men because all sinned—for sin indeed was in the world before the law was given, but sin is not counted where there is no law. Yet death reigned from Adam to Moses, even over those whose sinning was not like the transgression of Adam, who was a type of the one who was to come.

But the free gift is not like the trespass. For if many died through one man's trespass, much more have the grace of God and the free gift by the grace of that one man Jesus Christ abounded for many. And the free gift is not like the result of that one man's sin. For the judgment following one trespass brought condemnation, but the free gift following many trespasses brought justification. For if, because of one man's trespass, death reigned through that one man, much more will those who receive the abundance of grace and the free gift of righteousness reign in life through the one man Jesus Christ.

Therefore, as one trespass led to condemnation for all men, so one act of righteousness leads to justification and life for all men. For as by the one man's disobedience the many were made sinners, so by the one man's obedience the many will be made righteous. Now the law came in to increase the trespass, but where sin increased, grace abounded all the more, so that, as sin reigned in death, grace also might reign through righteousness leading to eternal life through Jesus Christ our Lord.

Romans 5:12–21

Here in the fifth chapter of the letter to the Romans the Apostle Paul is setting out a picture of human life as caught up in a great contrast between Adam and Christ. The contrast is between the first man and the last, between the first ancestor of the human race through whom it was corrupted, and the one through whom the human race is perfected. Adam and Christ are collective figures: They are not simply individuals in their own right, but rather they sum up humanity as a whole. Each forms one half of the contrast—between, on the one hand, the dark, destructive power of sin and unrighteousness, and, on the other hand, the omnipotent miracle of grace. For Paul, our lives and the lives of all around us are to be placed within this great contrast between sin and righteousness. In the end, all that really matters about human life in relation to God can be said by telling these two stories, the story of the first Adam who lays on us the curse of death, and of Jesus, the last Adam, the life-giving spirit (1 Corinthians 15:45).

We begin with the first Adam. "Sin," Paul says, "came into the world through one man, and death through sin, and so death spread to all men because all sinned" (Romans 5:12). Adam is the representative of human life under the dominion of sin, life under sin's rule. Three things need to be said about sin here.

First, sin is original. Original sin isn't something we invent each time we do it; it's already there, within us, deep in the structure of human life—in ourselves, and in humanity as a whole. There is in each of us, and in human life and history collectively, a depravity, a warping of our natures against God, something so basic and radical in us that we not only commit sins, but truly are sinners to the depths. Sin is original because it's the inescapable condition of human life which has broken loose with God.

It's important to grasp that to talk about original sin is not to suggest that some distant ancestor Adam failed and we are mysteriously infected with his guilt and curse. Original sin isn't a contagion or defect passed down through the generations of the human race until, finally, it reaches us and pollutes our lives also. If we talk that way, we all too easily make ourselves innocent: We're not really guilty, but just polluted—victims of Adam and not Adam's companions who willingly consent to Adam's crime against God. It's consoling to think of our sin in that way, simply because it lets us off the hook and holds another responsible for it. So Adam: "the woman whom you gave to be with me" is responsible for my sin (Genesis 3:12).

But this avoids the point of what Paul's trying to get across to us. There are no innocents; no one has an alibi, no one can shift the blame from themselves, even onto Adam. We're all implicated. There's an inevitability to sin, but it's not the inevitability of a disease passed down. Sin isn't a fate before which we are passive, nor an inheritance simply handed over to us. This is the inevitability of sharing in fallenness, sharing in human corruption, following and continuing that drive of human life away from God. We aren't just Adam's heirs, condemned for a crime we didn't commit; we're part of that great company at whose head Adam stands, the company of wretched men and women who have turned their backs on God. "All sinned" in the sin of the one man.

Sin is original; it's also deadly. Death came through sin, Paul says, and "spread to all" (Romans 5:12). Sin brings death because sin destroys that dependence upon God which alone gives life. We're creatures. We have our lives at the hands of God; "in him we live and move and have our being" (Acts 17:28). To live is to live in relation to God, to live in communion or fellowship with the one who is our beginning and our end. Life isn't our possession, something we own. We're alive as we receive life from

God, as the gift of his grace and mercy. God, the psalmist tells us, "holdeth our soul in life" (Psalm 66:9, KJV). But sin is the refusal to be held; it wrests free of the embrace of God. Yet free from God we're cut off from life-giving communion with God, and so we put ourselves in the realm of death. We take ourselves out of God's hands and place ourselves firmly in the hands of a ruthless and entirely successful killer. Or, as Paul puts it, sin always pays its wages, and the wages is death (Romans 6:23).

And third, sin is tyrannical. "Death reigned" (Romans 5:14); "death reigned through that one man" (5:17); "sin reigned in death" (5:21). Sin rules as a deadly tyrant. And so we suffer. We sinners are fools, and we're wicked toward others. But we also cause ourselves the unspeakable misery of putting ourselves in the power of a despot. We do it ourselves; no one else does it to us. We hand ourselves over to the tyranny of sin freely and willingly, because we foolishly think that this is a slight price to pay for what we hope to gain by wriggling free of the will of God.

Pretty soon, however, we find that what looked like open fields of liberty and fulfillment and mastery of our own fate are nothing of the sort. We find ourselves in a gray and cramped and rather frightening world, in the clutches of demons. We find ourselves trapped; we have been deceived into thinking that we are enhancing our lives when, in fact, we're binding ourselves to compulsion and falsehood and fear. Seeking to become gods and lords apart from God's gift of true life, we've become the bonded slaves of a lord who does not seek our good, and whose gift is not life but death.

This is the first story of human life, the story of Adam, the story of human life under the dominion of sin and death. Talking in this way isn't exaggeration. It's simply the repetition of the judgment of the apostle that, apart from Jesus Christ, sin and death reign with a terrifying effectiveness. Nor is it pessimism. It's rather the sober biblical realism which reminds us that apart from Jesus Christ we're sinners in a world of corruption, held in the grip of a master about whom we know only this: that he is utterly malevolent, that he will harm us now and forever.

If we remind ourselves of all this, it's not because we want to wallow in pathological self-accusation; it's because we need to face the truth. We aren't happy innocents who have got a bit lost in the woods; we aren't victims on whom truly sinful people trample. We're children of darkness (Ephesians 5:8); and there is no health in us.

But there is another way of telling the truth about human life. It's not a story of sin and condemnation and death; its theme is acquittal, and its conclusion is the gift of life. This is the story of the great reversal of all that's gone before: the overthrow of the order of sin and death, the casting down of the pretended lordship of evil, the setting up of the rule of righteousness. It's the story of salvation—the story of what Paul calls the "free gift" that's antithetical to the "trespass" (Romans 5:15), and identical with the name of the one man, Jesus. What are we to say about this second and last story? Once again, three things.

First, and most important, this story is preeminent, superabundant. It is *the* great reality. The two stories Paul is contrasting here—the story of sin and death, and the story of righteousness and life—are not dual aspects of the same reality, equal halves of a contrast. What is the balance of power between the first Adam and the last? The crucial phrase for Paul is "much more" (5:15, 17). How much more real and true and effective is the reality of Jesus Christ! His reality, the reality which he makes, is superabundantly real, real above all things. He isn't one more thing alongside sin and death, a little ray of light in the general darkness of the human condition. He isn't a solitary island of life in the midst of death. He is light. He is life. He is the death of death, the abolition of the rule of sin and the overthrow of its kingdom. He isn't merely the "second" Adam, following from the first but no more significant. He is the second and *last* Adam.

Jesus brings to an end the deadly reign of the story of the first Adam and makes all things new. Grace abounds (5:20). Grace—that is, Jesus Christ and the salvation of God in him—is limitless, undefeated, supreme. In the light of the grace of God in Jesus Christ, we know this about sin: In one very real sense, it is a finished reality, it has been dealt with, it's defeated. The first and the last thing that must now be said of us is this: We stand in the dominion of Jesus Christ, the kingdom of God and his Son, in which righteousness and life reign.

Second, therefore, the story of Jesus Christ means the triumph of righteousness. Jesus Christ is the "free gift of righteousness" (5:17) or "justification" (5:16, 18). The language is that of the law court. Paul uses it here to express the significance of God's great saving intervention in human life in Jesus Christ. Jesus is our justification or righteousness in the sense that he is our acquittal. Because of him, because of who he is and what he has done, we no longer stand under "condemnation" (5:16, 18). The guilty verdict which we'd drawn down on ourselves is removed, and we're declared free, finally and authoritatively.

So this isn't in any sense acquittal through moral performance, or a reward for good conduct. It's not something earned by years of carefully crafted holiness. It's a wholly "free gift," as Paul says five times in the span of three verses. Our justification is deliverance from a condemnation which is all too justly deserved, and which we can never hope to remove from ourselves. God does what we cannot do in declaring us righteous: Between us and the dreadful reality of our sin he sets the one great reality of Jesus Christ.

And so, third, the story of Jesus Christ means not death but "justification and life for all" (5:18). How? Because we're united to the indestructible life of Jesus Christ. In him we're delivered from the dominion of darkness and brought into his kingdom. His kingdom is the place of resurrection. United to him, we once again stand in fellowship with the life-giver, the one who has put death to death, who has brought life and immortality to light. The force of this for the Apostle Paul himself is hard to overstate: There is in his letters a deep sense of having been reprieved from a sentence of death, of having seen human condemnation disqualified by the incalculable mercy and goodness of God. Because Jesus Christ is, because grace abounds, then life will be the last word.

Such, then, is the great contrast which Paul draws here—a compelling and stark but above all unequal contrast between the first Adam, the figure of sin, death and condemnation, and Jesus the last Adam, the giver of life.

For most of us pondering this grand gospel theme, I guess it both does and does not make a difference in how we go about the business of our lives. We may be stirred by its force, or perhaps moved to see it as something ultimately true of us. Yet rather easily it seems a long way off; it seems a description of something that sometimes we can touch—if only just—but most of the time is out of reach. We don't feel delivered from sin and death, for they are our daily companions; we don't feel liberated from the old Adam, because we can recognize in him some very familiar aspects of our lives now. The gospel seems something splendid and potent, but not quite real. We may stand on the threshold of it all, but can't quite find our way inside. What are we to do?

One thing we might do is to try day by day to grasp something which is the simplest and yet the hardest thing for any of us to grasp: that the gospel is true; that growth in the Christian life is simply growth in seeing that the gospel is true; that Jesus Christ is the preeminent reality of all things. There's no technique here, no special insight for which we must hope, no extra illumination which we might expect. It's simply a matter of listening to the gospel often enough and hard enough until it comes to take up residence in our hearts and minds and desires. More than anything, we need to ask God to help us steady our lives around what the gospel declares to us: that we, the damned, have been delivered from hell, that we have been set free for life and liberty in the kingdom of Jesus Christ.

Tucked away in the Church of England's *Book of Common Prayer* is a little service for Ash Wednesday called "A Commination, or denouncing of God's anger and judgments against sinners" intended by the English Reformers as a Protestant alternative to public penance. It ends with this wonderful prayer, which we may make our own:

> *Turn thou us, O good Lord, and so we shall be turned; be favourable, O Lord, be favourable to thy people, who turn to thee in weeping, fasting and praying. For thou art a merciful God, full of compassion, long-suffering, and of great pity. Thou sparest us when we deserve punishment, and in thy wrath thinkest upon mercy. Spare thy people, good Lord. ... Hear us, O Lord, for thy mercy is great, and after the multitude of thy mercies look upon us; through the merits and mediation of thy blessed Son, Jesus Christ our Lord. Amen.*

CHAPTER 3

BELIEVE IN THE LORD JESUS

Acts 16:25–34

About midnight Paul and Silas were praying and singing hymns to God, and the prisoners were listening to them, and suddenly there was a great earthquake, so that the foundations of the prison were shaken. And immediately all the doors were opened, and everyone's bonds were unfastened. When the jailer woke and saw that the prison doors were open, he drew his sword and was about to kill himself, supposing that the prisoners had escaped. But Paul cried with a loud voice, "Do not harm yourself, for we are all here." And the jailer called for lights and rushed in, and trembling with fear he fell down before Paul and Silas. Then he brought them out and said, "Sirs, what must I do to be saved?" And they said, "Believe in the Lord Jesus, and you will be saved, you and your household." And they spoke the word of the Lord to him and to all who were in his house. And he took them the same hour of the night and washed their wounds; and he was baptized at once, he and all his family. Then he brought them up into his house and set food before them. And he rejoiced along with his entire household that he had believed in God.

Acts 16:25–34

Luke's account of the astonishing growth of the Christian community in the Acts of the Apostles is, at heart, a story about the unfettered progress of the good news. It sets before us the great theme of Acts, the unstoppable dynamism of the gospel about Jesus. At a number of points in Luke's story, the progress of the gospel is, quite literally "unfettered"—there are no fewer than three dramatic escapes from prison, of which our passage records the last. This particular episode comes in the course of Luke's narrative of the ministry of Paul and Silas in Philippi, which culminates in their deliverance and the conversion of the jailer. As in the other stories, so here: The apostles are imprisoned in a willful and wicked attempt to suppress the preaching of the gospel; they're liberated by spectacular divine intervention; those who witness the liberation are brought to faith, and the word of the good news once again triumphs.

Each of the stories gives a condensed version of how Luke understands the ministry of the apostles—as the progress of God's word of salvation through the world, overwhelming all opposition in the power of the Holy Spirit. And each of the stories offers us a little vignette of how Luke understands the gospel. Above all, each story gives us in dramatic form the essence of Luke's understanding of the gospel as concerned with *salvation*, with that passage from death and damnation to life and liberty which is God's accomplishment in Jesus Christ. Salvation, indeed, has been one of Luke's most basic themes in his two-part work, from the beginning of the Gospel of Luke, in which the coming of the savior is heralded as the coming of God's deliverance; through the ministry of Jesus, his dying and rising to new life; and on in the Acts of the Apostles, as the living Jesus makes his saving power known through his chosen witnesses.

And so here in Philippi, once again, we have the enactment of the same theme.

What Word of God do we hear in this story, and especially in the story of the conversion of the jailer?

Notice, first, how this story of salvation has at its heart a question: "Sirs, what must I do to be saved?" (16:30). Questions come in all shapes and sizes. What kind of question is this? It's an absolute question. It's not one of those questions which already contains within itself the germ of an answer. It's not a question that knows what to ask and expects a certain kind of reply. Nor is it a question that knows what it's after but needs some help in discovering where to find what it's looking for. On the contrary, it is a question which gives voice to absolute need: It expresses absolute emptiness. It's a question asked by someone with no resources, no clues, no hopes. Above all, it's a question in which, we might say, the one who is asking the question is himself absolutely called into question. In fact, we might say, it's not so much a question as a desperate cry for help. In effect, as Luke presents the story, it's the question of a ruined man. The jailer who throws himself on his knees and begs the apostles for an answer to his question is a ruined man, not only because he fears that he's lost his prisoners, his job and his life, but for an even deeper reason. He has witnessed the ruination of all human opposition to God. He has seen with his eyes the shaking of the foundations which comes about when the Word of the apostles' testimony to Jesus runs free in the world. He has found himself face to face with the extraordinary liberty of the Word of God which breaks apart all barriers. And so, he is ruined—called into question, judged, caught up in the conflict between God and sin, between the acceptance and the rejection of the message of salvation in Jesus. Hence, Luke tells us, he trembles with fear (16:29) and asks, What must I do to be saved? It's to that question—born of perplexity, born of the most profound sense of being dismembered by the events in which he is trapped, and not knowing where to turn—that the apostles' answer comes: "Believe in the Lord Jesus, and you will be saved" (16:31).

What is it that the jailer is told to do in answer to his question? Where does escape from ruin lie? It lies in a "name," and the name is the name of Jesus. Salvation—escape from ruination and destruction, and restoration to life and flourishing—is identical with the name of Jesus, with this one, the man from Nazareth, once crucified but now uncontrollably alive. Salvation, that is, is not some general idea, some generic religious reality. It's not something which comes in all sorts of shapes and forms, including a specifically Christian form. Nor is the name of Jesus a sort of label which Christians paste onto salvation, to give it a bit of Christian coloring. Salvation for Luke and for the New Testament as a whole *is* Jesus. He constitutes and embodies God's salvation.

Why? Because, the apostles tell the jailer, this Jesus in whom salvation is to be found is "Lord." He's the one in whom and as whom all God's purposes are brought about. He's the one in whom and as whom God rules all things. He is therefore the reality of God's saving rule. He's not some partial or incidental figure, some character on the margins of history, some territorial divinity. He is comprehensively Lord, Lord of all things. This Jesus—the one who has been glorified at his resurrection and ascension and now rules over all things at the right hand of the Father—this Jesus is *the great factor*. He is *the* reality of all human life; he alone is the reality of salvation. And so when the jailer turns to the apostles in the deepest distress and cries for help, what's offered to him is nothing other than a repetition of his name, a naming of this one, Jesus, as the one place where God's salvation is to be found. Believe *in the Lord Jesus* and you will be saved.

Face to face with this Jesus, the jailer is called to "believe." What is this belief to which he's summoned? Believing can mean something a good deal less than certainty. I believe the bus will come in five minutes, but I can't be sure. Or sometimes it can mean the kind of knowledge which is acquired after scrupulous review of evidence to build up a cumulative case for some conviction. But believing here is not half-certainty, nor the fruit of mental effort. It's belief in the deep, strong sense of giving allegiance to something which overwhelms us. To believe in the Lord Jesus in Luke's sense is to do far more than simply give him a passing nod with the mind or even to honor him with our religious devotion. It's the astonished business of being so overthrown by his reality, so mastered by his sheer presence, so judged by him, that we can do nothing other than acknowledge that he is supremely real, supremely true. To believe in him is to confess him—to affirm with mind and will and heart that he fills all things, that our only hope lies in his name.

Belief in this sense concerns the entire shape of a personal life. It embraces the whole of us. It's not one department of our life, something in which we engage alongside all the other things we do—working, loving, hoping, creating, worrying, and so on. Believing is about the way in which we dispose the whole of our existence. We believe when we're totally shaped by something outside of us, acknowledging that it has put a decisive stamp on all that we are and all that we do. This is why belief in this deep, strong sense defines us completely: We're "believers," doing all that we do out of the inescapable conviction that the Lord Jesus is the persistent factor in the whole of our life. Believing in him, confessing him, involves no less than everything.

And the issue of this confession of Jesus is salvation. "Believe in the Lord Jesus, and you will be saved" (16:31). It's very important that we get the connection right at this point. The apostles aren't saying, If you believe in Jesus, then as a reward for your belief you will be offered something called salvation. They aren't telling us that certain beliefs are a precondition, something we need to do in order to merit a divine gift: belief first, salvation second. No, they're telling us something incomparably more gracious than this. They're telling us that *as* we believe in Jesus, as we confess his sheer reality, we will discover that we *are* in the sphere of salvation. To confess him is to know that we are embraced by his salvation, taken up into that salvation and made new by it.

Our believing has no power of itself; we certainly aren't saved by belief. We're saved by the grace and goodness and majesty of him in whom we believe—by the one whom we confess as we believe. In a real sense, our belief is nothing in and of itself. It's simply a looking to him, a listening to him, in which we are wholly absorbed by that which we see and hear. To be absorbed in this way is *salvation*. Salvation is nothing other than the good order of human life as it is created and redeemed by God. To experience salvation is to be rescued from the unholiness of sin and to have our life reshaped, put into order, made new, so that we can be truly human. Being truly human in this way means being truly human in fellowship with God—not living in the darkness and ignorance and willfulness of life without God, but living out of a center in him, acknowledging him as Lord, and therefore finding in him truth, light, peace, goodness, order, and hope.

So much for Luke's story. What may we learn from all this? Maybe we can begin by acknowledging that we probably want to pull away from this kind of spectacular narrative of coming to faith. Many of us shy from identifying ourselves too closely with this sort of dramatic conversion story. We may associate it with shallow emotionalism, with those very visible and vocal forms of Christian discipleship with which many find it hard to identify themselves. We may find ourselves most naturally at home with a spiritual life which is quieter, more internal, more orderly and certainly a good deal less spectacular. Our instincts in this are, I think, often correct; we would be quite wrong to think that the conversion of the jailer represents an inflexible norm for how people come to faith. For many people, faith is just not something we "come to" in a dramatic, once for all event, associated with the breaking apart of the prison cell, literal or metaphorical.

But even if that's true for us—even if our spiritual life is more subterranean, less extroverted—nevertheless there is a permanent truth in this story of Luke's. That permanent truth is that all Christian life—however quiet, however restrained in its style—is born of *crisis*. It's born of a sense that there's something deeply wrong with human life; it issues from an awareness that our natural lives untouched by the grace of God in Jesus Christ are little short of a disaster. All Christian discipleship takes its rise from the jailer's question: What must I do to be saved?

Christian faith which does not have that as its constant preoccupation is quite far from the witness of the New Testament. There is, of course, considerable pressure to think of Christian faith in other terms. Perhaps we may like to think of it as concerned with morals, as a set of commands or imperatives which excite our best efforts at living the right kind of life. Or again, we may think of Christian discipleship as the cultivation of certain kinds of experiences, aesthetic or spiritual, or as the elaboration of certain ideas. Of course, morals and experiences and ideas are all very important. But we must also grasp that even good things can be used in such a way that they become evasions—they can so preoccupy us that they keep us from the heart of the matter. And for the New Testament, the heart of the matter, the heart of the Christian message, is constituted by a fearful question and a merciful answer: What must I do to be saved? Believe in the Lord Jesus, and you shall be saved.

There's a simple and definite challenge to us here. If we're not preoccupied by this question and answer, then we may be missing something of great importance to our souls' welfare. Yet there's also infinite and gracious consolation here—the consolation of the gospel which declares that Jesus Christ has died and is risen from the dead, and now stands in our presence, speaking his word of mercy and summoning us to share in his salvation.

To him be glory, now and forever.

CHAPTER 4

DEAD TO SIN

Romans 6:8–14

Now if we died with Christ, we believe that we will also live with him. For we know that since Christ was raised from the dead, he cannot die again; death no longer has mastery over him. The death he died, he died to sin once for all; but the life he lives, he lives to God.

In the same way, count yourselves dead to sin but alive to God in Christ Jesus. Therefore do not let sin reign in your mortal body so that you obey its evil desires. Do not offer the parts of your body to sin, as instruments of wickedness, but rather offer yourselves to God, as those who have been brought from death to life; and offer the parts of your body to him as instruments of righteousness. For sin shall not be your master, because you are not under law, but under grace.

Romans 6:8–14

ONE OF THE THINGS WHICH HAPPENS to us as we come week by week, Sunday by Sunday to the Lord's Table, is the inescapable reminder of our own sin. There's no point in coming here, no point in joining the line of those who go to the table and kneel to receive the tokens of mercy, unless we are somehow aware that we are defeated: defeated by sin, defeated by our own slide into routine wickedness, defeated by minds and wills which refuse to obey, and by bodies which all too readily become instruments of disobedience. If we take seriously what we are doing, then we have to see that we are about the bleak and humbling business of seeing ourselves as we are—not just as good folks who sometimes make a mess of life, nor even as bad people hiding a spark of native goodness, but as sinners: those who have offended not good taste and morals, but God.

Of course, the clever side of us tells us that all this is simply too morbid for words. Anybody, we say, who really feels the need to acknowledge and bewail their manifold sins and wickedness, or who thinks their sin is a grievous remembrance and an intolerable burden, is heading for self-destruction. There's a truth here: The soul which is driven by an accusing conscience and nothing more is in a perilous state. But the peril is not just that of an inflamed sense of sin; it's more that an inflamed sense of sin nearly always drives us inside ourselves, turns us inward. Consciousness of our own defeat at the hands of wickedness can all too easily lead us into that terrible situation in which we fall into the trap of thinking that we have to sort out the whole mess within the little orbit of our own lives. If there's to be any resolution to the conflicts of my moral life, if I am to break away from the destructiveness of sin, then the solution has to be within me. My efforts, my thoughts, my agonies of self-contempt and self-judgment, my striving—that's where the action must take place if I am to go to the Lord's Table acquitted and free and uncondemned.

And to all that, the New Testament, and especially Paul, and especially the Letter to the Romans, simply says no. There's no resolution to the conflicts of our lives within ourselves, no freedom from wickedness to be sought in striving, no peace with God which is the fruit of moral effort. And the reason why there is none is that we are, indeed, *defeated* by sin. It's not that we're occasionally overcome, or even that more often than not we lose the battle with ourselves. It's that we're *wholly* defeated, ruined; "there is no health in us." To look to ourselves, therefore, to try to sort ourselves out by doing an audit of our moral lives or a clean-up operation on our spirituality is, quite literally, a hopeless undertaking.

What, then, does the Christian gospel have to say to us? What hope does it hold out to those who are crushed by their sense of their own defeat? Well, in Romans 6 there's a rather strange sort of hope. It's strange because it comes in the form of a commandment: "Do not let sin reign in your mortal body so that you obey its evil desires. Do not offer the parts of your body to sin" (6:12–13). How on earth, we might ask, does that help us? How does it help us to be told that we must do what we patently can't do? Where's the mercy in being given yet another command that will defeat us and drive us further inside ourselves and our self-recrimination? The answer is simple—one little word: "*Therefore* do not let sin reign" (6:12). With that little word "therefore," Paul points to the amazing multiform miracle of salvation which he has so far been extolling in chapter 6 of Romans—the miracle that when Jesus died, our old, sinful, rebellious selves died with him, killed stone-dead by his cross; the miracle that when Jesus was raised to new life on Easter Day, we too were given a share in his new life free from the power of sin and death; in short, the miracle that we must (in Paul's words) consider ourselves dead to sin and alive to God in Christ Jesus (6:11). Because that is true—utterly and reliably true—*therefore* we are not to let sin reign. Here's the crucial point. We are not to let sin reign, we are to resist its power; but we mustn't do so in a fearful and anxious way, as if everything hangs on our effort, as if we ourselves have to put sin to death, as if sin's defeat is our business. No, we are not to let sin reign because in fact sin does not, cannot reign. Sin can be resisted because God has already dethroned it, stripped it of its power, defeated it finally and utterly at the death and resurrection of Jesus. Sin is not a powerful enemy now waiting for us to master it. Sin will have no dominion over us because it has no dominion over Jesus Christ. He is its master; dying, he defeats death, rising again, he triumphs over evil. And therefore, Paul tells us, we are able to say no to sin.

Now what is happening here? What's happening is this: Paul is trying to get us to see ourselves in an entirely new way. He's trying to get us to grasp the fact that what we strive so hard to accomplish has already been accomplished by God in Christ. He's trying to help us see that we are, as he calls it "under grace" (6:14). That is, the power which moves our lives, the ultimate driving force, isn't an awful demand, a miserable imperative that asks more and more of us and never relents in pushing us to perform. Rather, what moves us and makes us into the people we are is grace. And grace is a little New Testament shorthand word for the miracle of God's mercy in Jesus Christ. Grace has a name, the name of Jesus; he is grace, embodied and acted out: "For the grace of God has appeared, bringing salvation for all people" (Titus 2:11). To say that we are under grace is to say that the final truth of our lives, the final authority by which we are made and judged, is Jesus Christ the mercy of God.

If all this is so—and for Paul it is indeed so, astonishingly and liberatingly so—what does it mean for the shape of our living? There's a great deal that may be said, but one thing must suffice:

The basic commandment for Christian life is simply this, "offer yourselves to God" (Romans 6:13). Yielding to God is simply the practical expression, the living out, of faith. In essence, this means to let the truth of the gospel stand, let it be what it is, and be what it is for you. Negatively, this means a renunciation of all self-wrought attempts to establish standing before God by morals or spirituality or any other kind of uprightness. Yielding to God means giving up the whole enterprise of being my own maker, giving it up because it is the heart of sin, and giving it up because it is a ruinous affair, doomed to failure. Positively, yielding to God means coming to realize who we are, and living in the light of who we are. We're not simply the condemned who have to face the facts of their own betrayal and unworthiness and meanness of spirit. No, we're those, Paul tells us, who have been brought from death to new life (6:4). We've been raised from death, the living death of sin, and have been given a share in Christ's risen life. This is who we are, because this is who God declares us to be. And so we must live and act, with the permission and the freedom to be what God has made of us.

So when we walk to the table, and we receive the tokens of mercy, what does the gospel say? It doesn't say, Think the right thoughts, feel the right feelings, pray the right prayers. It says, "The saying is trustworthy and deserving of full acceptance, that Christ Jesus came into the world to save sinners, of whom I am the foremost" (1 Timothy 1:15). And it prompts us to make this prayer:

> *Grant us, therefore, gracious Lord, so to eat the flesh of thy dear Son, Jesus Christ, and to drink his blood, that our sinful bodies may be made clean by his body, and our souls washed through his most precious blood, and that we more evermore dwell in him, and he in us. Amen.*

CHAPTER 5

HE WHO COMFORTS

Isaiah 40:1–11

Comfort, comfort my people,
says your God.
Speak tenderly to Jerusalem,
and cry to her
that her warfare is ended,
that her iniquity is pardoned,
that she has received
from the LORD*'s hand*
double for all her sins.

A voice cries:
"In the wilderness prepare
the way of the LORD*;*
make straight in the desert
a highway for our God.
Every valley shall be lifted up,
and every mountain and hill
be made low;
the uneven ground
shall become level,
and the rough places a plain.
And the glory of the Lord
shall be revealed,
and all flesh shall see it together,
for the mouth of the LORD
has spoken."

A voice says, "Cry!"
And I said, "What shall I cry?"
All flesh is grass,
and all its beauty is like
the flower of the field.
The grass withers, the flower fades
when the breath of the LORD
blows on it;
surely the people are grass.
The grass withers, the flower fades,
but the word of our God
will stand forever.

Get you up to a high mountain,
O Zion, herald of good news;
lift up your voice with strength,
O Jerusalem,
herald of good news;
lift it up, fear not;
say to the cities of Judah,
"Behold your God!"
Behold, the Lord GOD
comes with might,
and his arm rules for him;
behold, his reward is with him,
and his recompense before him.
He will tend his flock
like a shepherd;
he will gather the lambs
in his arms;
he will carry them in his bosom,
and gently lead those
that are with young.

Isaiah 40:1–11

For the Christian reader of these great words, there is an especial resonance to Isaiah's declaration of the comfort of God. In the mouth of the prophet, they are, as best we know, a prophecy of the return of the people of Israel from exile; they point to the coming end of Israel's penal servitude, to Israel's forgiveness and restoration to fellowship with God. For the Church of Jesus Christ, these words are all this and more. Like the entire prophetic witness of Scripture, they have not only a backward reference to God's patient purification of a people for himself; they have a forward reference to that almighty act of God in Jesus Christ—to the coming of the Son of God, to a mercy which is *embodied*. For the Christian reader, therefore, knowing that these words are fulfilled above all in the Word made flesh, they point to a change in the fortunes, not only of Israel and Jerusalem, but of the whole company of humanity. They point to the limitless manifestation of the ruling grace of God in Jesus. And in pointing to that grace, they declare the boundless comfort of God.

Isaiah announces comfort, or strengthening consolation and consoling strength. What kind of comfort is this? It's a comfort *spoken by God*. For this reason it's of an entirely different order from worldly comfort. Worldly comfort takes all kinds of forms we can recognize in ourselves. It can take the form of the various hopes or aspirations or fantasies we dream up for ourselves when in trouble. We all, at one time or another, fall into this way of consoling ourselves, of making ourselves feel better despite harsh circumstances. We dream up consolation. But we know in our heart of hearts that dreamed consolation is no consolation at all, but a way of escaping from the truth without facing up to our disease or our distress. Imagined consolation changes nothing; it rather numbs us into avoiding what really is the case. Worldly comfort can also take the form of energetic action. We might comfort ourselves by attempting to change things, by struggling for a world that's more comfortable. Comfort then becomes something we can manage, an attainment within our sphere of competence: Work hard enough, live diligently in the right way, and comfort will be yours.

But Isaiah's comfort isn't fantasy, and it isn't a human project. It's that which God *speaks*. "Comfort, comfort my people, *says your God.*" We're hearing prophecy here, not mere human speech, not opinion, not aspiration, not pragmatic counsel, not a boost for morale. The prophet's voice, the tender cry to Jerusalem, is the speech of God himself; a voice speaking in God's name, by God's enabling, with God's authority. So Isaiah does not merely command comfort or recommend comfort; he *announces* it. God's own voice declares comfort—freely, with divine authority and force. What does this mean?

It means that in this matter of true human comfort, we enter a sphere in which God alone is competent. No mere human being can announce comfort of this kind; no one can take it upon himself or herself to declare what Isaiah declares. God alone may do this, because God alone is *savior*, and therefore comforter. With this announcement we're placed in the middle of God's work of salvation. We listen to an announcement that the human situation has been entirely changed—not modified or gingered up or temporarily cheered, but re-made, re-created. Salvation and its comfort are in the hands of God alone; all we may do in comforting is, as Isaiah does, testify to the miracle of God's mercy.

This comfort is God's comfort—God's to achieve and the prophet's to pronounce. And the essence of this true comfort, very simply, is *God himself*. The comfort for the people of God is not something alongside God; he himself is comforter and comfort; he himself is the consolation of Israel and therefore of the

Church. This comfort which God brings because of who he is, has three aspects: forgiveness, presence, and rule.

First: God's comfort is God's forgiveness. "Speak tenderly to Jerusalem, and cry to her that her warfare is ended, that her iniquity is pardoned, that she has received from the LORD's hand double for all her sins" (40:2). Sin is misery, because it's the perversion of our natures away from God. Sin deforms human life, which always leads to suffering. We cannot hope to despise God and his ways and remain authentically human—yet the singular history of the human race is that we do just that: break loose from God, tear up our roots in his life-giving presence, and then wonder why it hurts. Sin ruins us; and in ruining us it makes us guilty. It makes us feel guilty because we are guilty, our lives characterized by iniquity and lawlessness.

We desperately need pardon. We need to have the past erased. We need, somehow, to have sin dealt with so that it no longer controls us and makes the present the slave of the past. We cannot do any of this for ourselves. We know of no way out of hell. But God can do these things; God is capable of intervening in this sordid affair of our rejection of him. He alone is able to overcome our sin. We cannot pardon ourselves, though we would certainly like to do so and spend whole lifetimes trying.

We cannot put an end to the hard servitude to which sin condemns us. All we have—and all we need—is this single, commanding, definitive statement by God himself in Isaiah 40: The hard service of the guilty is over; iniquity is pardoned; the whole business of sin is over and done with, once and for all. This is God's comfort. It's not merely God soothing us, a palliative relieving only the symptoms of our distress. It's an entire alteration of our state before God, our *re-making*. It's the power of the creator set loose to save and to heal. God's comfort is forgiveness.

Second, God's comfort is God's presence. Isaiah's picture is of a royal visitation, sweeping everything away in its path, turning the whole world upside down. "Every valley shall be lifted up, and every mountain and hill be made low; the uneven ground shall become level, and the rough places a plain" (40:4) Why? Because "the glory of the LORD shall be revealed, and all flesh shall see it together" (40:5). God's glory is God's manifest presence. It is God's self-presentation—God with us, communicative, outgoing, resplendent. Isaiah's God is not remote, but is *visible*: "all flesh shall see it together." We ought not to get too hung up about the visible form of God's glory; what we must notice is its sheer reality. God makes his own way from himself to us; God *comes* to us.

God's coming is God's mercy, overcoming the alienation between us and God. His coming restores that life-giving fellowship with God in which alone we know what it is to be truly human. Sin pushes God out of the world; it hates God and will not abide his presence. Guilt longs for God's presence, but fears that his coming will only be destructive, and so it hides from him at all costs. But God's merciful coming pays no heed to sin and guilt; they are ruled out of court. God doesn't allow sin and guilt to keep him away from us; God comes. He comes as Israel is set free from exile and restored to fellowship; he comes above all in Jesus Christ. And in coming God evokes that most extraordinary human cry of amazement and joy in fulfillment of his promises: "Behold your God!" (40:9). In the face of Jesus God himself is made visible in his mercy as well as his glory (2 Corinthians 4:6). So God's comfort is his coming.

And, third, God's comfort is God's rule. "Behold, the Lord GOD comes with might, and his arm rules for him. ... He will tend his flock like a shepherd" (Isaiah 40:10, 11). That is, behold the one who comes with strong tenderness. He comes with might, rule, reward, recompense, establishing truth and justice with indefatigable power. And yet he comes as a shepherd, gathering the scattered and harassed people of God with infinite compassion. Notice how, as so often in Scripture, God's rule is the instrument of his nurture. The might of God isn't infinite energy which could break out anywhere and do anything; it's not a shapeless force. God's might is *God's* might, the infinite resourcefulness of the God of grace. God's power is shaped by his will; and God's will is always to be for us, never to be against us, always to be savior. That's why God's coming with might is gospel—good tidings, a matter for gladness rather than terror: "fear not" as you "behold your God" (40:9).

Once again, for the Christian reader of Isaiah there's a special charge here. The Christian has been given to know two things—first, that God has come definitively, unsurpassably, in Jesus Christ. What was hope to Isaiah is fulfillment to the Church. "We have seen his glory, glory as of the only Son from the Father, full of grace and truth" (John 1:14). "The only God, who is at the Father's side, he has made him known" (1:18). And second, the Christian has been given to know that in this same one, Jesus, the God who came will come again. Creation is not at its end; it's on its way to its goal, the great manifestation of God with us, of the fellowship of God with his creatures, secured through the Son, present through the Spirit, to be consummated at the Son's second advent. He will, we confess in the Nicene Creed, "come again in glory." And we shall see him as he is (1 John 3:2).

Such is Isaiah's announcement and its Christian gloss. It is, of course, is no distant announcement; it is our business, addressed to us. We would, no doubt, prefer to remain unaddressed; we would prefer not to have this strange and intrusive prophetic voice arresting our stately progress through life. But interrupt us it does, and we're to listen to what God has to say. We *must*—if we seek real healing. When we hear prophecy, we may not and must not treat it with cool detachment; prophecy isn't a matter for our appraisal but for our attention.

What God has to say to us is this: First, we are forgiven. Astonishingly, with no ground other than the miracle of mercy, the past of sin is over, and we are set free for holiness. Second, we live in the light of God's glorious presence. God isn't simply on the other side of the horizon. He is God with us, in Jesus Christ. Third, we live under his rule and therefore within his protection and care. He has taken away from us the evil responsibility we think we have for ourselves, and has set us under his might.

Such is the comfort of God; and in its light we may pray:

O God who didst promise that thy glory should be revealed, and that all flesh should see it together: Stir up our hearts, we beseech thee, to prepare the way of thine only begotten Son, and pour out upon us thy loving kindness, that we who are afflicted by reason of our sins may be refreshed by the coming of our Saviour, and may behold his glory; who with thee and the Holy Spirit liveth and reigneth one God, world without end. Amen.

Part II

THE SUFFERING SERVANT

CHAPTER 6

HEARING THE PASSION

Luke 23:26–30

And as they led him away, they seized one Simon of Cyrene, who was coming in from the country, and laid on him the cross, to carry it behind Jesus. And there followed him a great multitude of the people and of women who were mourning and lamenting for him. But turning to them Jesus said, "Daughters of Jerusalem, do not weep for me, but weep for yourselves and for your children. For behold, the days are coming when they will say, 'Blessed are the barren and the wombs that never bore and the breasts that never nursed!' Then they will begin to say to the mountains, 'Fall on us,' and to the hills, 'Cover us.'"

Luke 23:26–30

IT IS A FEARFUL THING to talk about and listen to the event of Jesus' passion. It is fearful first of all because the event of the passion is not something which we ought to *talk* about with fluency or ease. The terrors of the passion ought to lead us to silence rather than to speech, for words organize things, give them a shape, make them manageable. "It helps to talk about it," we say to the bereaved or the desperately ill. Words put things into sequences; we name what's going on and so give it a pattern, and make it less of a threat. But this of all events we can't manage. And though speak we must, our words can do nothing more than limp along, pointing out something which is not ours to make into just another bit of the world of which we've made sense.

The same thing troubles our *listening* to the story. We've heard the story countless times, and we have all sorts of ideas of how to interpret it. And because of this we may fall into the trap of thinking that we know what's going on here, and that we can allot it a place in our religious scheme of things and leave the story neat and tidy. This is exactly why it's very hard for us to hear what's being said to us. Our familiarity breeds not so much contempt as complacency: The gears of the liturgical year change yet again, we arrive at Passiontide, we know in advance what's going to be said, and so we forget to listen, we don't allow ourselves to be displaced or uprooted by what is set before us. Part of the struggle of reading the Bible during such times is the struggle to become real hearers of the words. The test of real hearing will not be whether we can conjure up the rather lush emotion which sometimes pervades this liturgical spell, but whether we let ourselves be told in no uncertain fashion that we are sinners, and that nowhere is this sin more visible than in Jesus' betrayal and death.

It is, moreover, a fearful thing to gather *in this place* and talk of the passion of Jesus. Here we are in the midst of a very solid piece of religious culture; everything about our gathering conspires to give us a sense of firmness and order. Our architecture and our music, the routines of liturgical and social form, the serious cadences of our language, all make for an imposing and weighty style of devotion. It's exactly this which brings many of us here: We look for the depth and enrichment which this gives to us; we are grateful for the way in which it releases us from constantly having to invent religious happenings. But religious culture always carries a temptation within it. The temptation is to incorporate the event of the passion within our religious culture—somehow to fix it, to make it comprehensible. Whether we do this through the measured prose of the *Book of Common Prayer* or the solemnities of Passiontide music, or the visual representation of the crucifixion at the high altar (now discreetly veiled), the effect can rather easily be to make the passion something which doesn't really cut us to the quick. Absorbed into our religion, it may be rendered something in-house, almost domestic. And if we are to hear what is being said to us, that must not happen.

We must not allow ourselves to make Jesus' passion into material for religion. In one very important sense, we aren't faced here with a religious event. It takes place outside the temple, outside the holy city, outside the gate, in the profane world. It's not a bit of cultic activity. Its chief protagonists are not the clergy fulfilling their official duties but unbelievers. Its place is in the shady world of political trade-offs and vacillating leaders and institutions hell-bent on survival. Making all this religious may miss what's happening, isolating it behind a sanitary cordon and robbing it of its capacity to interrogate. Most of all, the passion has little to do with the soaring of the religious spirit. Whatever else Passion Sunday may do, it lays before us that the gospel is not about the exaltation of the human spirit but about God's humiliation, God's entry into an ugly and irreligious bit of the world.

If all that's true, then we cannot consider Jesus' passion in this place without a certain ambivalence about the context and the manner in which we do so. This points to the fact that the passion of Jesus is concerned with *judgment*. "Do not weep for me, but weep for yourselves," Jesus says to the crowd as he is led away to his death (Luke 23:28). Why so? Why should we not weep for him? Ultimately, I think, because Jesus in his passion is not an object of pity. We know what it is to encounter the suffering of others, and to be moved by their plight, maybe even to tears. But even when we do weep for those who suffer, we do so most often from the relative safety of our own security and freedom from distress. There but for the grace of God go we. But, the story tells us, this is not our role here. We're not to think of ourselves as compassionate bystanders, looking on with sorrow as this poor unfortunate is maltreated and finally put to death. We may not console ourselves with the illusion that we are innocent, having no part in Jesus' betrayal and his being handed over to destruction. We must weep for ourselves. We must understand that by this event we are exposed and judged and condemned.

Jesus' passion shows us up for what we are. It's the hour of the world's judgment, because it is the hour when God lets the world have its own way. Here God lets the world be what it wants to be. God's judgment is, in part, God simply letting the world go, allowing the world to pull down the house on itself. God's wrath, spoken of with such zeal and torment in the psalms, is terrible precisely because God holds back his mercy, and doesn't restrain our zeal to wreck the world. Thus, the passion story tells us, have we made the world.

What kind of world have we made for ourselves? It's a world peopled by these kinds of figures. There is the outer circle, the crowd standing by, watchful, nervous, superstitious, no doubt including some who at one point or other were impressed with Jesus and followed him a bit but now keep their distance, shocked by their brush with his terrible fate. And then there is the inner circle of characters. The rulers, the religious authorities glad at last to be rid of a religious troublemaker, restored to the secure possession of their authority, able to indulge in the luxury of mocking Jesus who has finally turned out to be the bad business they always thought he was. There are the soldiers—coarse, brutalized, repeating without understanding the taunts of the rulers. There are the two wretched characters who share Jesus' fate: one in a rage of sheer terror, one overcome with shame. These, the story tells us, are the people of the world. This is what we look like when we come face to face with God. And this, moreover, is what we do with him given the chance.

Just so is our judgment announced. This is why we must weep for ourselves. The story of the passion shows finally and decisively what we are: We are at enmity with God, with one another and with ourselves. The scene is darkness visible, unrelieved, quite without nobility or grandeur, the revelation of the narrowness and meanness of human life that has broken free of the good order of God. We are *shamed*. We are shown the full extent of our guilt. We are forbidden any of those refuges to which we ordinarily turn. We may not turn to sentiment; we may not cast around for extenuating circumstances; we may not plead that we didn't know. We may not say that, in the same position, we would have tried to do differently—acted with less haste, with greater justice or wisdom, with less self-interest. Our only hope for escape is that we might somehow be able to flee from the awful revelation of our guilt by not existing, by asking that the mountains fall on us and the hills cover us so that God may not find us out.

So: The passion is the unbearable annunciation of the fact that we are condemned. And yet to finish here would be to miss the point entirely. The passion story certainly isn't something which we witness as spectators shocked by what others can do. But nor is it something which simply casts us into self-accusation. It exposes us to judgment; but it's precisely because of this that it's gospel, good news about salvation. How is this so? How is it that the King who does not save himself is truly our savior? How is it that our acquittal lies in the hands of the one who is here condemned? Very simply, we have to say something like this: The story of the passion, these few brief hours one afternoon in the history of the world, are the outworking of the eternal will of God for our salvation. Jesus' abandonment and death is not his defeat. It does not spell the overthrow of God's ways- quite the opposite. It's the fulfillment of those ways, the fulfillment of the eternal resolve of God to be our God, to take up our cause, to put an end to our opposition and establish our peace. "By oppression and judgment he was taken away," Isaiah tells us. "Yet it was the will of the Lord to crush him; ... he has put him to grief" (53:8a, 10). This is God's doing. This is not tragedy; it's not Jesus overtaken by a destiny which he could not master. It's the fulfillment in time of the eternal purpose of God.

As we say this, we must not somehow trivialize the passion, making it something cheerfully borne because part of God's plan. We must not lessen the sense which all the gospel stories present of Jesus caught, of Jesus' reduction to the status of object, of his passivity and apparent helplessness in the face of his tormenters like an animal caught in a net and powerless to flee. He's handed over, abandoned. Yet that abandonment is his giving of himself, not his giving up. It's at one and the same time his destruction and his triumph. It's the point at which the obedience of the Son to the Father is most real and most complete. And so it is the accomplishment of salvation. Other parts of the New Testament and the later Christian tradition will talk in many ways of that accomplishment—as a sacrifice, as a ransom, as a liberation of those in bondage, as an acquittal of the condemned, as the victorious overthrow of evil. But whatever image we may want to use, this at least we must say: that here is announced not only our utter condemnation but also its complete reversal, its abolition by God's grace. It is perhaps for this reason that Jeremiah's Lamentations is so meaningful. Lamentations is a great bleak poem on the judgment that afflicts the people of God when they turn from him. "The Lord is in the right, for I have rebelled against his word," the holy city laments. "He has cut down in fierce anger all the might of Israel...he has burned like a flaming fire in Jacob, consuming all around" (1:18, 2:3). And yet, judgment is mercy. In the revelation of our rebellion is shown also that this same God is the savior who is not defeated in our rejection of him, but who triumphs over us to give us life: "The steadfast love of the Lord never ceases; his mercies never come to an end; they are new every morning; great is your faithfulness" (3:22–23). We are to wait quietly for God's salvation; humbly, repentantly, keeping before our eyes the terrible knowledge of our rejection of God, but also setting our hope on the one whom we have rejected: "For the Lord will not cast off forever, but, though he cause grief, he will have compassion according to the abundance of his steadfast love" (3:31–32). May God give us mercy to hear these things.

CHAPTER 7

SIN SHATTERED WITHIN ITS STRONGHOLD

(Holy Week I)

Isaiah 52:13–15

Behold, my servant shall act wisely;
he shall be high and lifted up,
and shall be exalted.
As many were astonished at you—
his appearance was so marred, beyond human semblance,
and his form beyond that of the children of mankind—
so shall he sprinkle many nations;
kings shall shut their mouths because of him;
for that which has not been told them they see,
and that which they have not heard they understand.

Isaiah 52:13–15

TWO THINGS BY WAY OF INTRODUCTION to this series of four homilies in Holy Week.

First, our task as we listen to and reflect upon the Word of God in Holy Week is very simple: We must give attention to Jesus Christ as he sets himself before us in Holy Scripture. Whatever else we may do this week, in prayer or penitential reflection and self-examination, this above all we must do—we must *listen*. When we do that, when we listen to the Bible in Holy Week as at any other time, we are placed in the presence of Jesus Christ. As we hear Scripture read, we are in the presence of one who speaks to us by his Holy Spirit. These ancient texts are not curios, little windows on an antique religious culture into which we peer from afar. They're the speech of Christ to us. He, the living Christ, present among us in the Spirit's power as we assemble in this place, is the one who speaks. He is not distant, and he is not mute. He comes to us and addresses us by this creaturely servant, the ancient texts of Scripture through which he speaks his living word of judgment, forgiveness and consolation that is new every morning. We listen to Scripture as the living voice of the living Christ.

The task of listening seems simple enough; we know the story pretty well, most of us, and have some ideas about how to make sense of it. But in fact the listening required of us is terribly hard—above all because we don't *want* to hear. We're sinners, estranged from the one who speaks here, and what he has to say to us is alien to us. We don't want to be spoken to by this one; we don't want his intrusive voice. Why is it that so often we go away from Scripture unmoved, unaffected, dull? In the end, it's because we refuse to be schooled by Christ. We don't want to give our mind and affections to what he has to say to us.

Because this is so, if we are to hear this prophecy, then something has to happen to us, something has to be given us from outside to heal us. If we're to become listeners, then we have to be cleansed; something in us has to be put to death, something new has to be created—the capacity and desire to give attention to God. Hearing Scripture requires conversion, regeneration: It can work properly only when we have been made new by God. And yet, we cannot make ourselves new; nor can we somehow produce the skill of listening to this particular Word out of the store of our innate capacities for language and understanding. If we're to be made capable of listening to God, the Spirit of God must act upon us and in us. Here, then, is spiritual work to be done not *by* us but *to* us, *for* us. God in his mercy must make us hearers of the Word.

The second thing to say at the start is that our thoughts will be focused on the passage from Isaiah 52 and 53. It's one of the passages from Isaiah which have become known collectively as the Servant Songs, because they speak of a strange figure referred to by the Lord as "my servant" (52:13). Who this Servant-figure is remains shadowy in the prophecy. At various points in Isaiah, the identity of the Servant seems to shift. At first, it seems as if the Servant isn't an individual but a corporate reality, some special group within Israel. Later, the Servant becomes increasingly an individual figure. By the time we get to our text, we're pretty clearly dealing with a particular person.

Who this person is never becomes plain in Isaiah; but two things do become clear. First, the Servant seems to be the central figure in the drama of God's grappling with his people. The fate of the Servant as it were condenses and focuses the struggle between the Lord of the covenant and his wayward people. Second, the Servant suffers, and this suffering is in some way God's appointed means both for Israel's reconciliation and his Servant's own exaltation. The Suffering Servant is thus called by God to a particular office or place in the life of God's people, and in that office at one and the same time he bears the truth of Israel's sin and is himself the divine instrument of its overcoming.

From very early on in the Church's history, Christian believers looked to these texts from Isaiah, above all chapter 53, as they struggled to map out for themselves their explosive conviction that Jesus was Messiah, the embodiment of God's salvation. Partly this meant that the figure of the Servant in Isaiah offered them a figure of great resonance and depth through which they could try to speak of the significance of Jesus. Partly, also, it meant that Christians read Isaiah in the light of Jesus' unsurpassable reality. It's not so much that Christians came to think of these passages in Isaiah as directly predictive prophecy, every statement neatly fulfilled in a particular aspect of the ministry of Jesus. It's more that Christians confessed that Jesus Christ is the center of reality, the core of all things and their fulfillment. All history, all experience, including the history and experience of Israel, is grounded in him, and in him is manifest the central truth of all human life that God is the reconciler.

On the basis of this conviction, Christians read the Old Testament as part of the story of God's dealings with humankind culminating in Jesus. And so they took passages like this from Isaiah and said, in effect, the reality of which these passages speak is nothing other than the reality manifest in Christ. Whether Isaiah meant to foretell in detail the ministry of Jesus in these Servants Songs does not matter in the end; the key thing is that what Isaiah has to say finds its fulfillment in Christ. And so for the Christian reader, Isaiah and every other part of Scripture speaks of Christ, for Christ is the sum and substance of God's dealings with humankind. But not only does *Isaiah* speak of Christ; Christ *himself* speaks of himself through Isaiah. By faith we acknowledge that the Servant of whom we read is none other than the one who now addresses us as Lord.

What do we read? We hear God addressing Israel with these words: "Behold, my servant shall act wisely; he shall be high and lifted up, and shall be exalted" (52:13).

My Servant shall act wisely, and ultimately, *prosper* (see 53:10–12). This is almost certainly not where we would begin to think about Holy Week! By venerable tradition, our meditations in Holy Week have become suffused by a kind of penitential gloom, with our thinking focused on the suffering and death of the Lord, and upon contrition for our sin that caused his fate. None of that, of course, is inappropriate or unworthy. But they aren't the place to begin, and our pondering of the passion will be disordered if we start there.

Why must we not begin with the suffering of Christ? Why must we start at the seemingly opposite end—with his exaltation, his being lifted up? Very simply because the point of the whole story of the passion is not loss but *triumph*. These few days into which we now enter are God's victory.

The picture of the Servant of God Isaiah unfolds is by no means a picture of unresolved evil. It's not simply an account of sorrow and wretchedness unleashed upon the Servant. Certainly it includes the wounding and oppression of God's Servant. He is indeed a man of sorrows; he is acquainted with grief; he is despised; he is taken away, and put to death by the wicked. But none of that is sheer, unabated suffering. The Servant's suffering is the strange manner in which under the hand of God he prospers; it's the path along which he is lifted up and reaches his exaltation.

Jesus' whole ministry, from start to finish, from Bethlehem to Golgotha, is the royal progress of the Son of God. It's an undefeated act of lordship. Even in Holy Week, or rather *especially* in Holy Week, he is lifted up and exalted. Of course, his progress involves an encounter with fundamental opposition; it involves his rejection; it involves the repudiation and demonization of his proclamation; it involves his being despised; it involves the perversity of his being cast out from God's people and put to death outside the gate. Jesus was indeed marred beyond human semblance, his form beyond that of the sons of men (52:14). But he was not a victim. Jesus wasn't overwhelmed by an alien fate. He wasn't overpowered when he was put into the hands of others. He is the Son of God in majesty; He is the Lord God in the flesh, suffering others to do this not out of weakness but because he bends even our wickedness to serve his purpose of reconciling us to himself.

As we read the stories of this last week of the life of Christ, therefore, we are not to think of what we read as the last days of a good man scandalously treated and slowly engulfed by powers too great for him. No, we're to wonder at the majestic condescension of God, the unbroken movement of the will of God. At the Last Supper, faced with the presence of his betrayer, Jesus said, "the Son of Man goes as it has been determined, but woe to that man by whom he is betrayed!" (Luke 22:22). These words—"as it has been determined, but woe"—stand over the whole of the course of the passion. Holy Week is no accident and no tragedy. The betrayal of Judas, the abandonment of the disciples, the vacillation and weakness of Pilate, the self-protection of the leaders of the people—none of this corners Jesus or overtakes him. He is and remains Lord.

Why is it so important to emphasize this? Why is it so important, that we're dealing with Christ's *exaltation* here? Ultimately, it's because Holy Week is about the world's salvation. Holy Week is the climax of God's dealing with human wickedness, the point at which sin is dealt with once and for all. Sin cannot be overcome simply by the pathetic image of a suffering man. Sin cannot be eradicated merely by God offering us a picture to ponder with empathy or even appreciation, the picture of Jesus as despised and rejected. God does not deal with our sin by inflaming our pity. God deals with sin by a majestic act of limitless divine power and effectiveness, which is no less truly human for being so.

God *himself* intervenes. In the person of his own Son, he shatters sin from within its stronghold in human life and establishes the final rule of salvation. He "shall sprinkle many nations" (52:15). If this isn't so—if Holy Week isn't the Lord God himself facing his and our enemies and overthrowing them—then all is an empty show, whether it evokes our sorrow and compassion or not. If that's all God has for us, then there is no mercy, no grace, no forgiveness, no rebirth. We're left to ourselves to try and unmake our own ruin. Yet the word of the gospel is that we're not left to ourselves. With God there is mercy; with the Suffering Servant there is grace. This is the good news proclaimed to those who have never heard anything like it before (52:15). And mercy and grace are simply summary terms for what happens in the rest of this Servant Song: God's Servant is afflicted and taken away; yet in that affliction he bears our iniquities and sorrows. And thus God's Servant is high and lifted up.

CHAPTER 8

LIFTED HIGH IN HUMILIATION

(Holy Week II)

Isaiah 53:1–3

Who has believed what he has heard from us?
And to whom has the arm of the Lord been revealed?
For he grew up before him like a young plant,
and like a root out of dry ground;
he had no form or majesty that we should look at him,
and no beauty that we should desire him.
He was despised and rejected by men;
a man of sorrows, and acquainted with grief;
and as one from whom men hide their faces
he was despised, and we esteemed him not.

Isaiah 53:1–3

We turn our thoughts for a second time to the song of the Lord's Servant in Isaiah 52–53. In company with Christians down the ages, we read this passage of Scripture—like every passage of Scripture—out of the fact that for us, the center of Scripture is Jesus Christ. Because we confess Jesus Christ is Lord, and everything is rooted in him, then Scripture, too, in all its parts is a testimony to the gospel of Christ. That means two things for how we read the Bible: that we read everything in the light of Christ, and we read everything in order to discern the light which it sheds on Christ. And so Isaiah is about the gospel—not because whoever wrote Isaiah knew this, of course, but because the living Christ chooses now to declare himself through Isaiah's words, to announce his gospel to us.

Yesterday when we began looking at this passage from Isaiah, we saw how the presentation of this strange and shadowy figure of the Servant of the Lord begins in a very specific place—not from humiliation, but from exaltation. The heart of the story is not the Servant's oppression, but the fact that as he does his work and discharges his office, he *prospers*. And, moreover, we saw how crucial this exaltation or prospering is for our understanding of the decisive final events of the ministry of Jesus which are at the center of our attention in Holy Week. The passion of Christ is not fate, not accident, not tragedy. It's the majestic progress of the Son of God as he strides to glory, as he is exalted and lifted up.

Yet his exaltation includes his humiliation. The particular form of his majesty is this: that he should give himself into the hands of the wicked, that he should become of no account, that he should be counted worthless. It's to this that he *gives* himself. But, we must see, he gives himself to *this*. He does not give himself up, and he does not give himself away. This is what he chooses; this is the direction of his freedom; this is the Servant's glory. Yet what is it that he gives himself to? What are we to make of the strange form of his glory?

First, in the strange form of his glory the Lord's Servant gives himself to contempt: "he was despised, and we esteemed him not" (Isaiah 53:3b). What that means is this: He exposed himself to the way in which we sinners organize the world around values that we've made up. We go through our lives as if we were kings, bestowing our favor on things and people as if the very fact of our favor made something valuable. We make desire, not truth, the real clue to what's valuable. If we desire something, then it has value; if not, we despise and reject. And in the person of his Son, the Lord God himself enters into this perversity of ours. In the man Jesus, he comes to us with nothing to recommend himself. He has no form or comeliness or beauty, none of those natural endowments which attract us and which we think valuable. He does not present himself in such a way that he fits in with our desires. Judged by our standards, he is nothing. And so he is despised; indeed, we hide our faces from him so that our world can remain intact. And who does this? We do. We despise, and reject, and esteem him not.

Second, in the strange form of his glory the Lord's Servant gives himself to betrayal. There are many betrayals which accompany the Son of God in these last few days: Judas, seemingly cold, calculating, tough; Peter, muddled, cornered into those few words which destroy his entire world: "I do not know this man" (Mark 14:71). Betraying follows pretty easily from despising. It's no great leap from thinking that someone is worthless to betraying them, because to betray someone is to refuse to acknowledge and live out the claim that that person has. Betrayal means that, faced with opposition or temptation or ridicule, we fail to stand by a commitment to another. It's another instance of that vicious lack of integrity which afflicts human life and fellowship—we make promises but break them; our word is not our bond; our fidelity is worthless. And this, too, turns on the Son of God; into the midst of this, too, he places himself.

Third, in the strange form of his glory the Lord's Servant gives himself to suffering oppression in silence. "He was oppressed, and he was afflicted, yet he opened not his mouth; like a lamb that is led to the slaughter, and like a sheep that before its shearers is silent, so he opened not his mouth" (53:7). As the story of the passion proceeds, Jesus retreats into a terrible silence. Throughout the rest of his ministry, he is a commanding speaker: He speaks his Word, and the world is remade; his Word brings judgment, renewal, healing, consolation; as he speaks he brings to his hearers the authority of truth; he is the eloquent presence of God. But in his passion, he withdraws more and more into saying little or nothing; before his oppressors, he is dumb. Why the silence? It's not that his silence signals his defeat—as if he is no longer able to speak his Word of power. It's more that his silence is his holding back, the willed restraint in which voluntarily he takes on the office of sufferer, freely giving himself into the hands of his oppressors, literally letting them have their say. "This" says Jesus to the little mob who come to get him, "this is your hour, and the power of darkness" (Luke 22:53). He, Jesus, permits this hour to be; he is not its victim. But in permitting it he gives himself to be taken away by oppression and judgment.

Fourth, in the strange form of his glory the Lord's Servant is "cut off out of the land of the living" (Isaiah 53:8). Despised and betrayed and silenced, he is murdered. He *has* to be killed. There's no other way to end his claim on us. He has to be eradicated, because we know in our heart of hearts that unless he is, we cannot remain intact in the way we want to be. Jesus' ministry is characterized by a potent refusal to let us be in our own way—by an insistence that if we are to live in the truth, we have to face the reality of God, God's mercy and God's claim. He, Jesus, the Lord's Servant, bears to us this mercy and this claim; in him it is utterly and insistently and inescapably present. And it's for just that reason that he must go. He has to be put out of the world because we are not safe with him around. He will not leave us alone; he is the truth and speaks the truth (John 14:6), and of all things, that is the last thing that we want. We do not want this man, because we do not want this God. And so what do we do? We repeat the history of sin which has been the same from the very beginning. We decide for ourselves that God's claim is worthless; we tell ourselves that we know better; we treat the truth of God with contempt; and when God comes to us, we reject, and afflict, and strike out. All this, Isaiah tells us, is the office to which the Lord's Servant is appointed; as such a one, he is to prosper. And so "they made his grave with the wicked" (Isaiah 53:9).

Such is the form of the glory of the Lord's Servant, the strange path which the Son of God is ordained to follow. And such, too, is the final demonstration of who we are. We are those who do this. It's very easy to hear the events of the passion and think of those who did these things as demons—utterly wicked, evil beyond belief. But it's not so. Those involved—the oppressors, the betrayers, those who despised Jesus—are not examples of some titanic evil; what they do is by no means out of step with what we would do and what we actually do. Their sins are the average sins of the average person. In doing what they do, they simply follow the perverted course of all our lives. They are not monsters; they are human beings like us, and their lives are in direct continuity with our own. It may console us to think that we would have done otherwise—that we would not be oppressors and betrayers, that we are not so depraved. But what we have before us is nothing other than the history of all of us; and, as such, it leaves not only them but us without excuse.

Why are we without excuse? What is it that is so appalling about the oppression and betrayal and putting to death of Jesus, the Lord's Servant? It is the fact that we're rejecting *him*. The rejection of Jesus is not only one more crime against humanity. In rejecting him, we are not only rejecting a human neighbor, a fellow human being for whom we are in some measure responsible and toward whom we are to required act with justice. We're rejecting the Lord God. In the person of this one, we despise and betray and oppress and put to death the Son of God himself. That's the core of the wickedness here. We reject the one to whom we are absolutely obligated, to whom we are inescapably bound. The Son of God is not another neighbor whose claims we can weigh up for ourselves and either accept or reject. He's not one who leaves us free to choose whether we will acknowledge him or not. He is God's claim. He is the Lord. He is the God of the covenant, in whom we are determined, who has already made a decision about us. The folly and wickedness of Holy Week is just this: that we try to overturn his decision, try to make him into nothing, and so bring the house crashing down on ourselves.

Yet we may not end there. However mean and dreadful our wickedness may be, it does not have the upper hand. What these people do, and what we do in them, is caught up within the purpose of God. Oppression, betrayal, affliction, murder, become reconciliation. Here, too, the Lord's Servant prospers. The deepest affirmation made in the next few days is not that we are sinners but that God bends even our sins to his purpose. We think to humiliate this contemptible Servant. But through that God exalts him, lifting him up and making him very high. We do not of ourselves understand how this can be so. We understand only if God, as Isaiah puts it, *reveals his arm* (53:1). That is, our knowledge of these things is his gift, and therefore we must pray, and wait, and listen, so that he may instruct us.

CHAPTER 9

TAKE THIS HOLY SACRAMENT

(Holy Week III)

Isaiah 53:4–5

Surely he has borne our griefs
and carried our sorrows;
yet we esteemed him stricken,
smitten by God, and afflicted.
But he was wounded for our transgressions;
he was crushed for our iniquities;
upon him was the chastisement that brought us peace,
and with his stripes we are healed.

Isaiah 53:4–5

ALTHOUGH IT MAY SOUND a bit odd to say it this evening of all occasions, Maundy Thursday is not really at the center of our understanding of what we are doing when we gather together and celebrate the Lord's Supper. The story of the last gathering of Jesus with his little band of disciples is, of course, pretty central to the liturgies we use. They all include in one form or other a recital of that story as what liturgically minded folk call "the institution narrative;" and they do so because Maundy Thursday constitutes the point at which, according to Archbishop Cranmer's prayer, Jesus "did institute and in his Holy Gospel command us to continue a perpetual memory of that his precious death." The Church doesn't celebrate Communion because it thinks this is a good idea, or a handy piece of ceremonial, but because on this night—the same night that he was betrayed—Jesus commanded the Church to do so.

But Maundy Thursday is meaningless without what follows on the next day of passion week. The memorial which is instituted tonight and which we are commanded to continue is a memorial, not of the Last Supper, but of his death. Maundy Thursday is about Good Friday. And to continue week by week, day by day, to celebrate the Lord's Supper is to lodge at the heart of the Church the single fact of the death of the Lord.

This means, immediately, that there is an inescapable *backward* reference in every act of gathering for the Lord's Supper. The Christian Eucharist is a memorial. But what is a memorial? Clever theologians sometimes take me to one side with a kindly look in their eyes and explain to a poor benighted Protestant like me that in the Bible remembering doesn't mean calling to mind something past, but rather means reactivating or reenacting the past so that it's powerfully present among us now. But though I'm open to argument, I don't in the end think that's really right. It's not right because whenever we start talking in terms of making something present, we cannot avoid taking away from the uniqueness and unrepeatability of what happened on the cross. What we do when we gather for Holy Communion is not a re-enactment; it is looking back to what took place once and for all.

The cross of Christ, the old *Book of Common Prayer* tells us, is full, perfect, and sufficient; it doesn't need prolonging, re-enacting, or reactivating. It is the one single, complete fact in which God deals with the sins of the whole world. It stands. It is finished. Celebrating Communion is thus not first of all about here and now, but about there and then; only because it's about there and then is it about here and now. That's why Paul calls it a proclamation of the Lord's death. We don't proclaim the Lord's death by sacramentally making it real, as though it were not real to start with. We proclaim the Lord's death as, by the grace of God's Spirit, we attend to what took place then, in that place, with that little group of participants and the larger crowd of onlookers, and, at the center, the Lord's Servant. Holy Communion proclaims the Lord's death as it testifies to, points to, indicates, what was done once when Jesus the Servant of the Lord was put to death.

What was done there and then? What is it about the Lord's death that the Eucharist proclaims or testifies? Isaiah, whose Servant Song provides the bass line of our thoughts this Holy Week, tells us that the wounding and bruising and chastising of the Servant is "for our transgressions" (53:5). The cross of Jesus, celebrated in Holy Communion, is the climactic event in which God acts to win the world back from the darkness and misery of sin. In some way, the death of this one changes the entire course of human history; it intercepts and breaks the whole course of human wickedness; henceforth, because of what this man does and suffers, nothing can be the same. Why not? Because in this little scrap of an event one Friday afternoon, this unremarkable bit of human evil, God takes our place. He enters without reserve into the reality of our situation—into our situation, that is, as those who have damned ourselves, who have cut ourselves off from life and put ourselves into hell, all because we made up the lie that we can be human without God.

But God does not leave us in the hell we have made for ourselves. In the person of Jesus his Son and Servant, he comes to us; he takes on his own back the full weight of our alienation and estrangement; he freely submits to the whole curse of our sin. He takes our sin upon him, and in so doing he takes it away, fully, finally, and conclusively. And of all that—of that miracle of grace on Good Friday—this evening is a memorial, the memorial of that his precious death.

That was what was done. It was done not by us, but by God himself in the person of his Servant and Son. And it was done by God alone. Because reconciliation is thus God's work, God's *exclusive* work, then this sacrament in which we remember the cross of Christ is also God's work. Here, in this assembly at this table, God is at work. And God's work here is to present to us, to make present to us, what took place on Good Friday. We don't make Good Friday real by re-enacting it, or by thinking and feeling about it. God in this sacrament declares to us what Good Friday made true: that he is our reconciler; that sin is finished business; that we *can* repent because God has forgiven; that the promise acted out in the death of Jesus stands for all time and for each human person. In this memorial, God turns us backward; but he also makes present to us the limitless power of what the Son of God suffered. The God who was at work there and then is at work here and now, proclaiming to us his promise of cleansing, acceptance and peace.

What then do *we* do now, as we assemble to remember? In one very real sense, we do nothing. That is, whatever we do does not in any way contribute to or supplement or finish off or make real what God has done. Once again, the words "it is finished" (John 19:30) stand over the whole of human reality, the whole of the Christian life, including our celebrating the Lord's Supper. What we do is therefore a strange kind of doing. It's doing in which we don't initiate, don't try to bring something about, don't try to make the world. It's a doing in which we receive and take into ourselves the gift of what God has already done. And that doing is called, very simply, faith. We often get a bit messed up about faith, because we think it must be some activity of our own—maybe a set of ideas to which we cling on tenaciously, maybe a psychological state we hope to induce, maybe a set of contrite feelings, maybe a great exercise of our wills. But in the end you can't reduce faith to those things—ideas or feelings or acts of will. Faith is not first and foremost a matter of what I do or what I am; it is not at heart me striving to be something. In faith we look beyond ourselves and our works and simply acknowledge and rest in something other than ourselves—the utter sufficiency and provision of God. Faith lets God be God, lets God do God's work.

And so when we gather for a celebration of the Lord's Supper, it is faith which is basic to our response to God. By faith we hear God's Word in Scripture, testifying to the good news of Jesus Christ. By faith we look to God who has absolved us from our sins. By faith we take the tokens of God's loving promises. "Take and eat this in remembrance that Christ died for thee, feed on him in thy heart by faith with thanksgiving." We don't need to be righteous; we don't need to have the right doctrines or emotions; we don't need to make great acts of moral commitment. We don't need anything—which is the same as saying that what we need is faith, resting in who God is and what God does.

Who is this God who waits for us at his table? The God who in the person of his Son and Servant bore the sins of many and made intercession for the transgressors. The God who has made many to be accounted righteous. And so, draw near with faith, and take this Holy Sacrament to your comfort.

CHAPTER 10

THE TRIUMPH OF DIVINE RESOLVE

(Holy Week IV)

Isaiah 53:6, 10

All we like sheep have gone astray;
we have turned—every one—to his own way;
and the Lord has laid on him
the iniquity of us all.

It was the will of the Lord to bruise him;
he has put him to grief;
when he makes himself an offering for sin,
he shall see his offspring, he shall prolong his days;
the will of the Lord shall prosper in his hand.

Isaiah 53:6, 10

We end these thoughts on Holy Week where we began—with the central truth that what has taken place in the week that has passed, and what has taken place supremely at the event of the crucifixion, is the outworking of the will of God. To the participants and bystanders, no doubt, everything seemed very far from that, just another muddle in a place inflamed with strife. And to the followers of Jesus, the little ragtag caravan of men and women who found themselves attached to him, it was nothing short of disaster. Yet Isaiah speaks of the putting to death of the Lord's Servant as God's will—as the outworking of the eternal purpose of God, as no accident but rather the place where we are to learn to see God's resolve, undeflected, undefeated, utterly effective. How can this be so? What is this divine resolve which is set before us here, in the affliction and grief of the Servant of God?

It is the eternal resolve of God to be our reconciler. What is enacted in this miserable little drama is God's plan and purpose to live in fellowship with us—God's will that he will be our God, and that we will be his people. Fellowship with God is what human beings are for. That is, we flourish as human beings if we live in free and joyful and humble relation to God. To be human is to be in relation to God—and that relation to God is not a sort of added extra, something to supplement our lives. It is the core of being human; it is the way in which we are properly alive. We are alive and truly human as we live in and from that fellowship.

For this fellowship God makes us. But at the core of Scripture's presentation of this fellowship is the devastating fact that it has broken down: The life-giving bond between God and his human creatures has been smashed into pieces; we have chosen to try and live outside fellowship, and so estranged ourselves from God.

Fellowship is replaced by alienation, God's friendship with God's wrath. Isaiah puts it thus: "we have turned—every one—to his own way" (53:6). That is, there has been a great turning in human life, not a turning toward God but a contrary turn, a swerve away from God and toward ourselves, a veering away from fellowship and toward a way of living which is of our own making. We choose what Isaiah calls "our own way." We choose, that is, to live in the world as if we could make up life as we wished, as if there were no script, as if there were no order or structure or given reality, no shape but what we invent. Indeed, at heart, that's what's happening: We are inventing ourselves; we are becoming our own makers; we are deciding that we do not want to be the creatures of grace. We are asserting that we possess ourselves—and not only ourselves, but the whole world—and that we will live as we please. We devastate ourselves by lawlessness: not just lawlessness in the sense of breaking the rules, but lawlessness in a deeper sense—the terrible disorder which afflicts us when we no longer live in the form that we have been given by God, and in companionship with God, but instead take to ourselves the rights and dignities of being our own creators. The fruit of that disorder is that we "go astray"—that human life becomes scattered, rootless, homeless, at odds with itself because it is no longer fixed to God.

All this is what we make of ourselves. It is our iniquity, our transgression. And it is our misery: We get what we want. We want life without fellowship with God, and that is what we get—only instead of giving us life and freedom, it turns out to lead to our destruction. We make ourselves; and precisely in making ourselves, we destroy ourselves. Now the passion of Jesus Christ, the Son of God and the Lord's Servant, is the way in which God says no to this whole chaos which we have unleashed on ourselves. At the cross of Jesus Christ, God arrests the whole course of our sin; God sets aside finally, once for all, the entire mad project in which we try to be our own masters; God overthrows sin. God does not leave us to our own devices; God refuses our refusal of him; above all, God maintains and re-establishes with us that fellowship in which alone we can live and flourish. God alone can do this. We cannot help ourselves. But God can, and does, come to our assistance. In the situation of our absolute jeopardy, in our desperate peril, God comes to our side. And God does it in this way. He takes our place. He himself assumes the role of the human partner who has broken away from God. He himself, the Lord God, in the person of his Son, enters into the estrangement and enmity which we have made for ourselves; he becomes one of us. As Isaiah puts it, in the person of his Son and Servant, God himself is "numbered with the transgressors" (53:12). God takes flesh, our fallen, sinful, accursed existence as sinners, and takes our lot upon himself.

He becomes, that is, the bearer of our sins. "Surely," Isaiah tells us, "Surely he has borne our griefs and carried our sorrows" (53:4); and again: "the Lord has laid on him the iniquity of us all" (53:6); and again: "he bore the sin of many" (53:12). It's easy to misunderstand this. If we're not careful, we can think that what's happening in the passion is that God is simply punishing an innocent victim for our wrongdoings—as if God simply requires that the punishment for our crimes should be enacted, and it doesn't matter who is punished. But Jesus is not just a mute sacrificial animal. If he is like a lamb led to the slaughter, it's not because God is victimizing him; it is because he is God himself fulfilling his own purpose; it is because he is God the Son, freely and lovingly acting out the will of the Father. "It was the will of the Lord to crush him" (53:10). That does not mean that God just vented his anger at sin on Jesus. It means that he, Jesus, the Son of God, is God himself bearing the wounds of our wickedness. God does not save us by sacrificing someone other than himself. God sacrifices himself. In his Son, God himself bears our sins. He makes himself an offering for sin (Hebrews 7:27). Or as Colossians puts it "in him"—Jesus—"all the fullness of God was pleased to dwell, and through him to reconcile to himself all things, whether on earth or in heaven, making peace by the blood of his cross" (1:19).

How does this change the course of human life? In this way: By becoming one of us, by absorbing into himself the full extent of our sin, God destroys sin. God sets aside a whole world, the world we have made for ourselves, and God puts in its place a new world, the world of the new creation. In that world, we are set free from sin, and set free to live in fellowship with God. Good Friday, and its final outworking on Easter Day, is the new creation, the re-creation of the world. It's the point at which the world and all humankind are made new. We can't do this; we can't undo the knot we have tied. But God can: God has power and authority to make new, and in the passion of his Son performs this ultimate act of mercy, bearing our iniquities and so setting us free. And for us, this means that we become *righteous*. That is, we are put back in relation to God. Fellowship, friendship with God, is restored—not by us, but by God himself. We no longer turn to our own way; God himself turns us back to himself.

Good Friday is thus the triumph of grace, the triumph of reconciliation over enmity, the victory of life. On this day, in the hand of Jesus the Son and Servant of God, the will of the Lord prospers.

We may not, however, leave matters there. For these things of which we read and speak are not the business of other people only; they are our business. These matters concern us. The Lord has laid on him not just others sins, but sins of us all, and therefore our sins. What took place there and then is comprehensively true; its claim and its effectiveness are universal; none of us is free to think that we are passed over in this affair. The gospel addresses each of us: "You, who once were alienated and hostile in mind, doing evil deeds, he has now reconciled in his body of flesh by his death" (Colossians 1:21–22a). If that's true—if it really is true that in the passion of Christ God has reconciled us to himself—then the most basic task of human life is simply to acknowledge that this is so. We are not at enmity with God; we are not trapped by wickedness; we are not under condemnation; we are reconciled to God. Part of us, of course, refuses to acknowledge that, because we don't want to be reconciled to God. We prefer, still, to turn to our own ways. However absurd and lifeless and hurtful it may be for us, we prefer to pretend that we are not reconciled to God. Another part of us dare not acknowledge that we of all people are reconciled to God; we cannot conceive that the gospel can be so good that it will deal with our sins, too. But the unbelief or guilt or fear that holds us back counts for nothing. God has taken from us the power to live apart from him. We will not stop him prospering. The Lord's Servant will see his offspring. And of all that—that unbelievably gracious promise—Easter Day is the promise and security. Jesus Christ, God's Servant, reigns—at his cross, and on the day of his resurrection, and now as he is preeminent in all things. And that is why we call this Friday good.

Part III

HEARING GOD

CHAPTER 11

LISTEN TO HIM

Mark 9:2–10

And after six days Jesus took with him Peter and James and John, and led them up a high mountain by themselves. And he was transfigured before them, and his clothes became radiant, intensely white, as no one on earth could bleach them. And there appeared to them Elijah with Moses, and they were talking with Jesus. And Peter said to Jesus, "Rabbi, it is good that we are here. Let us make three tents, one for you and one for Moses and one for Elijah." For he did not know what to say, for they were terrified. And a cloud overshadowed them, and a voice came out of the cloud, "This is my beloved Son; listen to him." And suddenly, looking around, they no longer saw anyone with them but Jesus only.

And as they were coming down the mountain, he charged them to tell no one what they had seen, until the Son of Man had risen from the dead. So they kept the matter to themselves, questioning what this rising from the dead might mean.

Mark 9:2–10

The story of Jesus' transfiguration on the mountain is a rather odd bit of the Gospels' presentation of him. Many of us don't feel at home with this kind of story. This is hardly the stuff of everyday life; it's all too fantastic—mythological, perhaps—and certainly very far from the world we find ourselves in. So what do we do with this strange material?

Maybe the first thing we need to say is this: It's precisely because we do find it odd and embarrassing that we should take it with great seriousness. It's precisely because we can't make much of it at first that we need to attend all the more to what we read here. Reading the Bible isn't about confirming our ideas and experiences and going away satisfied. It's about being challenged, called into question. Part of the point of the Gospel stories is to upset our habits, to set before us something utterly different from our world, to push us into thinking about something absolutely new. We aren't the judges of Scripture; it judges us. Its task is to astonish us; it doesn't say to us what we want to hear, but says to us what must be said if we are to hear and respond to the truth of the gospel. What does this story of the transfiguration set before us? What surprising new reality does it ask us to face?

Mark sets before us the manifestation of Jesus' glory. Jesus is radiant with the glory of God. God's glory is the sheer splendor of who God is: "I am the Lord; that is my name; my glory I give to no other" (Isaiah 42:8). It is God's majesty, the amazing beauty of God, the extraordinary brightness of who God is. His glory isn't something hidden, tucked away in heaven far from us: "Out of Zion, the perfection of beauty, God shines forth" (Psalm 50:2). God's glory shines; it fills the world; it makes itself known to us. God's glory is God encountering us, God coming out to meet us. Thus the psalmist declares that "our God comes" (50:3).

God's glory is God's presence; it's the astounding fact that God, the majestic one, the Lord of all things, is God with us, God for us, God who sets himself before us so that we may know and worship him. And where does this happen? Where do we encounter the glorious presence of God? For Mark, as for the other gospel writers and for the New Testament as a whole, we encounter God's glory here, in this one, in the face of Jesus Christ (2 Corinthians 4:6). He, Jesus, is the glory of God; he, Jesus, is the glorious God who comes to us and meets us and invites us to see himself.

Now, it's crucial for understanding the story of the transfiguration to realize that the glory which is revealed here isn't merely an episode in the story of Jesus. It's something true of the whole of who he is, of all he does. The glory of God in Jesus Christ suffuses the whole of his life and ministry; here in the story of Jesus on the mountain, it becomes visible in a special way. In other words, what Mark is pointing us to isn't an odd little incident in the story of Jesus. He is trying to tell us about something quite basic: Jesus shares in the glory of God. Whatever else we make of what happens here, it's about the way in which Jesus participates in the unfathomable light of the being of God. This is no temporary occurrence, a spiritual high which Jesus experiences, only to pass away as life returns to normal—not at all. What happens on the mountain is the revelation of who Jesus really is, "the radiance of the glory of God and the exact imprint of his nature" (Hebrews 1:3). Who is he? The one who shares God's glory. He is God's likeness.

Here we reach something quite fundamental to Christian belief. At it's simplest, the Christian confession is that knowing God and knowing Jesus are inseparable. What it means to be faced with the reality of God is bound up with what it means to be faced by Jesus. Jesus is not just a pointer to God; he is not just a messenger telling us something about God; he is not just a prophet calling us to respond to God. Rather, in seeing him we see God (John 14:9); in his acts we see God's acts (John 9:4); in his words we hear God's Word (John 12:49). He is God's presence. And so he is God's glory. Jesus is not like a mirror, reflecting a light from outside; he is himself the glory, the one who is the radiance of God. God from God, we say in the creed, Light from Light, true God from true God.

This is not an abstract point, which makes no practical difference. Everything hangs on it. If it is not true—if Jesus isn't God's glory—then the Christian faith simply crumbles. What's the heart of the Christian confession? Here in Mark's story it's contained in the words coming from the cloud which descends on the scene: "This is my Son, my beloved" (9:7). The cloud indicates the presence of God himself, the holy one, the Lord (for example, Psalm 97:2). And the words repeat what was said by the divine voice at Jesus' baptism: "You are my beloved Son; with you I am well pleased" (Mark 1:11). They're the words of God in which we are told who Jesus is: the Son of God, God himself present and active among us as Lord and Savior. And they are the words of God which mark Jesus out; here we are told that he, Jesus, is the one upon whom the Father's favor rests in an altogether unique and unrepeatable way.

Why does this matter? Why does it matter that Jesus is God of God, Light of Light, very God of very God? Very simply, it matters because it's true. It matters because it is *this* God and no other who is set before us in the gospel. It matters because there is only one God, the one who takes flesh and comes among us, and we behold his glory, the glory of the only-begotten Son (John 1:14).

So much, then, for Mark's story. What does this glory of God in the face of Jesus Christ require of us? What difference is it supposed to make to us if we take seriously this miracle of divine radiance? The first thing that ought to be said is that we need to realize that taking all this to heart is a disturbing business. It was certainly disturbing for the Apostle Peter. True to fashion, he started babbling away, trying to organize this miracle into some interesting religious event where he could play his part and find himself useful—let's set up a shrine, let's try to fix the moment, let's get going with religion (Mark 9:5, 6)! Peter missed the point. Faced with the transcendent glory of God in Jesus, what's required isn't talk or religious business. What's required is silence and inactivity. What does the divine voice tell us? Not "here's the raw material for a cult;" not "here's an experience to cultivate." Instead, what we are told is, "This is my beloved Son; *listen to him*" (9:7). We're commanded to listen. Listening here means a lot more than casually tuning in for a moment or two before we switch off again. It means real listening, intense listening, listening which hurts. It means attentive straining after what is said, giving ourselves wholly to the task of attention to Jesus. Why? Because he is God's Word, he is what God says to us. In him and as him God makes himself known to us as the light of the world. Listen to him.

Such listening is to be the basic dynamic of our lives. It is, of course, to be basic to our gathering for worship as well. As Christians get together on the Lord's Day, the chief task is to hear what God says to us. We seek to hear God in the reading of Scripture; we seek to hear God in the visible words of the sacraments; we seek to hear God in the words of our neighbors and fellow-Christians. But listening to Jesus is not only a religious business. It is a way—*the* way—of being human.

Listening means obedience, and obedience is not craven submission; it's not born of fear. Obedience to God is the lifelong task of giving my consent to the shape which God has for my life. Obedience is letting God put me in the place where I can be the sort of person I am made by God to be. I come to see what that kind of person this is when I stop trying to be in charge of myself, and instead acknowledge that God is my Lord, that I can only be myself if I walk in his ways. So listening to Jesus is always a practical matter, a matter of living the life which God gives me, being what I am called by God to be. And in its simplest form that call of God is this: "Listen to him."

We need to be very honest at this point. We find this listening virtually impossible. Try as we may, we end up in failure. We get distracted; we find our hearts are not moved by the desire to listen to Jesus; we prefer listening to others, or to ourselves, or to nothing. The whole thing seems insuperably difficult. Many Christians are crushed by a sense of inadequacy in their Christian lives, ground down by a sense that they simply aren't good enough. What help is there?

The help is this—God helps us in our incapacity. God enables us to listen to his Son. God makes it possible for us to see the glory of God in the face of Jesus Christ, to long for it, to desire it more than anything, to live our lives by it. And God does so by giving us faith. But believing is not simply what we do; faith is God doing something to us so that we can see him and know him and love him. Faith is not my work (Ephesians 2:8). Faith is not the capacity to believe things without evidence, or a great flood of emotion in which we lose touch with real life. Faith is what happens when my life is knocked down, bowled over, by the dazzling, marvelous reality of God in Jesus Christ.

With the same faith, we're invited now by the risen Jesus to eat at his table, humbly, repentantly, knowing that we wouldn't and shouldn't be here if it were not for his mercy. Draw near, then, with faith. Listen to him. Receive his body which he gave for you and his blood which he shed for you. Eat and drink in remembrance that he died for you. And feed on him in your hearts by faith with thanksgiving.

CHAPTER 12

PRAISING GOD

Psalm 95:1–5

Oh come, let us sing to the Lord;
let us make a joyful noise to the rock of our salvation!
Let us come into his presence with thanksgiving;
let us make a joyful noise to him with songs of praise!
For the Lord is a great God,
and a great King above all gods.
In his hand are the depths of the earth;
the heights of the mountains are his also.
The sea is his, for he made it,
and his hands formed the dry land.

Psalm 95:1–5

Psalm 95 (the "Venite") has been part of morning prayer since the very beginning of Anglican public worship in the 16th century. Those early Anglicans did not, however, invent this custom; the first Anglican prayer books are simply continuing an ancient Western Christian tradition which goes back at least as far as St. Benedict in the first half of the sixth century. It's sometimes called the "invitatory psalm" because of its place at the beginning of morning prayer as an invitation to worship. The psalm may have begun life in temple worship in ancient Israel, though we know very little about its original context. Its function in Anglican morning prayer is, however, very clear. It is one of the two opening moves in the Anglican service of mattins which function as a prologue to what is going to happen in the rest of our gathering for public worship.

The first of these two moves is the little set of what are called "versicles and responses" with which the service opens:

O Lord, open thou our lips
And out of our mouth shall show forth thy praise;
O God, make speed to save us
O Lord, make haste to help us.

They are rather easily passed over as we clear our throats at the beginning of the service; but notice what's really happening there: The words are a prayer, a prayer to God that he will do for us what we simply have no hope of doing for ourselves—namely, opening our mouths to praise God as he is to be praised. They are a prayer for God's enabling. And because of that, what lies behind the prayer is a recognition of our incapacity; an acknowledgement that in the matter of worship we have no resources and will fail miserably unless God speeds to us and makes haste to help us. Worship is that in which God and God alone must save us and come to our aid. In this matter, as in all things, we must wait upon God's deliverance.

All this is then picked up in the second opening move in the service of mattins, which is Psalm 95. The opening versicles indicate that worship is a place of supreme need in human life; the psalm goes on to tell us that worship is also a place where we are exposed to a real and serious conflict. The conflict is a conflict with ourselves. It tells us that what makes worship such a difficult business for us is not just our incapacity but our unwillingness: We do not want to worship; we do not care to listen to this God; we do not desire to come into his presence; we will not render him praise and thanksgiving. Psalm 95 falls roughly into three sections: a first section, the first five verses, which exhorts us to enter in joyful worship of God; a second section, verses 6–7, which speaks of God as our God, the God who has chosen us for fellowship with himself and the God to whom we must listen; and a final section, verses 8–11, which warns against hardness of heart by looking at example of the children of Israel in the wilderness. So we have an invitation to praise God; an affirmation that we belong to God; and an exhortation to obey God.

Having the Venite right at the beginning of morning worship gives us a basic picture of what's really going on when we gather together. Christian worship is a gathering with a very definite purpose and a gathering in which a very specific event takes place. Its purpose is that we should encounter God. Worship is not an indefinite matter, a space of time for us to fill up as we choose. It is encountering the Lord, coming into his presence, kneeling before him, finding ourselves before his face. And the very specific event which takes place in Christian worship is the event of turning from sin to the reality of God. What happens in worship? At the most basic level what happens is that we enter the presence of God. And as we enter God's presence we are called to set aside disobedience and to hear God; to set aside our coldness and rebelliousness and to rejoice in God; to abandon unbelief and to praise God. Christian worship always involves conversion. It involves permanent, continual conversion of our lives, a radical change which accompanies every act of worship and every worshiper. No gathering is immune from this; no congregation—however pure or committed or orthodox—is ever free of the demand for conversion. If we approach the worship of God thinking that we have put this behind us, then we have not even begun to understand what worship is about. This dynamic—this conflict between praise and hardness of heart—is the core of what we are about today and every time we worship God; it is *today* that we are to hearken to his voice.

Psalm 95 is an invitation to worship. But the worship to which it invites us is not private but public. The psalm is addressed to the people of God in their common life, and the worship to which it summons us is worship in assembly: Let *us* sing; let *us* rejoice; "let *us* worship and bow down; let *us* kneel before the Lord, our Maker!" (95:6). The worship of God is principally a public activity; it is an action in community. Why? Because I do not worship *my* God, but *our* God; God is my God only insofar as he is the God of God's people. It is this principle, of course, which informs something close to the heart of the Anglican tradition, namely the importance of "common prayer." The core of that tradition is what Thomas Cranmer in his invitation to morning prayer called "assembling and meeting together." What builds up our common life as the people of God is public obedience to the summons of the psalm: Come, let us sing to the Lord.

To say this is not to deny that worship is also a private and individual matter. Every person has business to do with God, and no one else can do that business for us. Without roots in private prayer and seeking God's face, without pondering Holy Scripture and examining ourselves, the life of faith is simply a shell. Indeed, however much we may value public worship, we can use it to hide from God. Nevertheless, the accumulated wisdom of the Christian tradition is this: Assembling and meeting together is basic to the rhythm of the life of faith. It is not an option, something which we can drop in and out of as the fancy takes us. It is what God requires, and it is what builds us up. Our culture very easily relegates religion to solitude; it tempts us to replace worship by spirituality, and to think that the life of faith is just self-cultivation, growing a more interesting me. And to that we Christian folk must politely and firmly say, quite simply, no. God is honored by obedience to his command; and his command is that—however unappealing it may be—we must give ourselves to the public praises of his people.

Now, how are we to set about this task of worshiping God? Two things.

First, worship involves a movement in a very definite direction. "Oh come" (95:1)—we are invited; and "Let us come" (95:2)—we enter into worship by making a movement. Worship involves us in turning from one set of preoccupations, from one sphere of activity and responsibility, and directing ourselves toward another sphere. We are to turn in the direction of the presence of God himself. We are to direct ourselves toward him, to turn and place ourselves before the face of God. We do not make this move unaided—indeed, we cannot; but by the empowering of God himself, we are enabled to bend our lives toward the sheer reality of God. The Hebrew word in the psalm here conveys a measure of haste and urgency: This coming to God is not a gentle stroll; it has the speed and application of those attending to the most serious and pressing business. As we do that—as we turn to God with energy and deliberateness and exclude all distractions—we are not, of course, saying that all other concerns are of no value. The primacy of worship does not consign everything else to the rubbish heap. We are not forced to choose between "worship" and "life." But we do have to see that unless we make this move in this direction we will have no grasp at all of what to do in all the other movements of our lives. Unless we turn to God, unless that fundamental movement is a regular and steady part of our lives, then the rest of what we do will be a jumble of activities without coherence and without orientation.

Worship involves an urgent turning to God. Second, worship involves a measure of intensity. "Let us make a joyful noise to the rock of our salvation!...let us make a joyful noise to him with songs of praise!" (95:1–2). If the psalm does reflect the kind of worship which took place in the temple, then it's obviously got something pretty exuberant in mind: a cheerfully noisy and undignified procession of voices and instruments heading for the courts of the Lord in Jerusalem. Lots of Christian congregations have rediscovered this kind of exhilaration, of course, and worship with an exuberance which makes some of us look pretty staid. But exuberance is only one kind of intensity. There is also an intensity which is quiet and restrained and undemonstrative but which is no less caught up in the movement of worship. What's crucial is that worship should arise from and give voice to deep joy in God. The roots of worship are love for and delight in God and the ways of God. Exhilaration there may be; but what matters above all is focus, a fixing of heart and mind on the face of God. "What is it to rejoice aright?" asks St. Augustine; and his answer is: "To rejoice in the Lord." If we sing, we are to sing *to the Lord*; we are to come into *his* presence; we are to make a joyful noise to *him*.

With this we reach the heart of what's being set before us in these first verses of the psalm, which is, very simply, God himself. What draws forth the movement of worship? God himself. And what evokes the intensity of worship? Again: God himself. And so our final task is to spend a moment looking at how we are to characterize the reality of God which lies at the heart of our public praises. Four things are to be said.

First, most generally and comprehensively: God is worshiped because he is "a great God." Worship is acknowledgement. It is recognition of the absolute superabundance and the limitless majesty of God. Worship is without measure, because God is without measure; there can be no end to our praises, for there is no end to the divine glory. Worship recognizes the supreme worth of God. It is the astounded cry which is drawn from us when we know ourselves to be in the presence of the one who sums up in himself all goodness, all truth and all beauty. Worship is the repetition and celebration of the utter fullness and aliveness and holiness of God. In the end, worship says only one thing: God is God. God is this one, supremely great. Worship doesn't ascribe anything to God; it is not a statement of the value that we think God has. Nor is it flattery, hoping somehow to win favors. Worship acclaims that from all eternity, in all his ways and works, God is the perfect one.

Second, and more particularly: God is worshiped because he is incomparable. He is, the psalm tells us, "a great King above all gods" (95:3). That doesn't mean that there are in fact lots of gods around, and that the God whom we worship just happens to be the best of the bunch. It certainly took the biblical tradition quite a bit of time to sort this point out, and the way the psalm phrases the point might lead us to think of God as a kind of hyper-god—immensely exalted, but nevertheless one of a class. But what that sort of statement is reaching toward is the deep idea of God's incomparability. God's majesty, that which we worship in him, is such that it is beyond compare. God needs no competitors to display his supremacy; he is not bigger, stronger, more exalted, because he is outside and above any such associations. He is simply and staggeringly himself, unique, the one before whom everything else fades, the one whose glory is different not just in quantity but in quality from everything else. And it is this one, the psalm tells us, that we worship: no deity of our making, dreamt up to satisfy our needs, but this one—the one who is *above*.

Third: God is worshiped because he is the governor of all that he has created. "In his hand are the depths of the earth; the heights of the mountains are his also. The sea is his, for he made it, and his hands formed the dry land" (95:4–5). God is creator. That is, he alone has done what no creature can do: make something out of nothing. He alone does this, and in the light of what he does, all our engineering of the world looks pretty trivial, merely rearranging the furniture of the universe. And as creator, God is sustainer. What God's hands have formed, God's hands hold; all that is continues to be and reaches its goal because God moves it and God shapes its ways. Again, our self-important pictures of ourselves as holding the destiny of nature in our hands are shown to be faintly ludicrous. We can but scratch the surface; it is in God's hands alone that all things are grasped, and so it is God alone who is the object of our worship.

Fourth and last: This God—the great one, the one beyond compare, the God of creation and providence—is our God. He is the rock of our salvation. He is not mere cause or force, not simply infinite power. He is God with us and for us and so—astonishing as it must seem—our God. And so, "let us worship and bow down; let us kneel before the Lord, our Maker!" (95:6).

People end up in church for all sorts of reasons: sometimes because of habit, or from curiosity; some may have a half-glimpsed need, some may be very aware that they have to do business with God. But over and above all those assorted reasons for ending up in this place at this time, we need to try to grasp what is really going on here. We are in God's presence; here God speaks his Word to us; here he makes himself known. We may have stumbled into all this by accident rather than design, but that is where we are. We are caught up in the chief work of God's creatures, which is to worship him. It is a work which flows into all other works, the works of the mind and the heart and the hands. But whatever else fails, this work, the work of public worship of almighty God, must not fail. If we would have all things to go well for us and our neighbors, we must continue in this task. Left to ourselves, failure is inevitable; left to ourselves, we do not have a hope of answering God's call to kneel before the Lord our Maker. But we are not left to ourselves. We are in the hands of God. The risen Jesus Christ is with us; the Holy Spirit of God is in us. And because that is supremely true, our worship will not be empty but fruitful, and will take us to the courts of the Lord of hosts. And that is why we pray:

> *Almighty and merciful God, of whose only gift it cometh that thy faithful people do unto thee true and laudable service; Grant, we beseech thee, that we may so faithfully serve thee in this life, that we fail not finally to attain thy heavenly promises; through the merits of Jesus Christ our Lord. Amen.*

CHAPTER 13

BELONGING TO GOD

Psalm 95:6–7

Oh come, let us worship and bow down;
let us kneel before the Lord, our Maker!
For he is our God,
and we are the people of his pasture,
and the sheep of his hand.
Today, if you hear his voice
do not harden your hearts, as at Meribah.

Psalm 95:6–7

THE PSALMS ARE an incomparable treasure. They are one of the most powerful instruments through which God shapes our unruly minds and affections. In a unique way, the psalms school us in the life of faith. Here in the psalms there is laid out before us a sort of spiritual anatomy of the people of God: what gives them joy, what causes them to stumble and sin, what makes them suffer, what makes them praise God in the midst of suffering, and, above all, what kind of God is present with them and sustains them in the life of faith with mercy and correction.

In his commentary on the psalms, Calvin says this:

> What various and beautiful jewels are contained in this treasury, it were hard to find words to describe ... I call this book ... "The Anatomy of all the parts of the soul," for not an affection will man find in himself, an image of which is not reflected in this mirror. Nay, all the griefs, sorrows, fears, misgivings, hopes, cares, anxieties, in short, all the troublesome emotions with which the minds of men are often agitated, the Holy Spirit has here pictured to the life.

It is my experience that those words of Calvin ring true; and I have become more and more persuaded that there is no better way of deepening our knowledge of the spiritual life than pondering the psalms day by day, year by year, until they become part of us. Listen hard, and the psalms will take up residence in you and become the very stuff of your lives. And with that, we turn again to Psalm 95.

As it sets out the grounds on which God is to be worshiped, the psalm moves from the most general to the most intimate. It begins, that is, by giving the most general reason for the praise of God, namely God's greatness. It then moves more specifically to emphasize God's incomparability: God is to be worshiped because he is the one who is above all other so-called gods. Next, it moves one step closer by directing our attention not simply to God in himself but to God in relation to the creation: God is worshiped not only because of his intrinsic worthiness, but also because he is creator and sustainer, the one who forms and holds all things. "In his hand are the depths of the earth; the heights of the mountains are his also. The sea is his, for he made it, and his hands formed the dry land" (Psalm 95:4–5). And last, this movement toward the realm of humankind is brought to a climax as the psalm announces that God is to be worshiped, not only for his intrinsic greatness, not only for his transcendence of all other heavenly powers, not only for his work as creator and supporter of all that is, but because *he is our God*.

Why are we to worship, to fall down and kneel before the Lord? Because of the supreme fact that God's works and ways include this astonishing fact: that he is our God, and we are his people. Worship is rooted in *covenant*, in the *covenant fellowship* between God and the people of God. What's involved in making sense of this? Why is the covenant between God and his people so crucial in grasping what is happening in our worship?

The existence of the people of God is something *strange*. The coming together of God's people is not a natural but a supernatural event. Why is it strange and supernatural? Because the dynamic of the coming together of the people of God is not in itself. What brings these people together is not a purely human movement; rather, it is a divine work—a divine calling or summons. Other human gatherings have at their heart the will to assemble, to get together for some common task, to build a common life in order to achieve a common purpose.

But matters are not so with the gathering of the people of God. The people of God are not just one more human group, one more self-directed form of common human life. Of course, the people of the world may think that that's all there is in the people of God—they may think that the people of God are no different from any other human assembly. And we ourselves are often enough tempted to think that, because we don't look all that different from all the other kinds of human common enterprise; the Church is just another natural collection of people with a common aim. But it is the consistent witness of Holy Scripture that this is not so. If there is a people of God, if there is a coming together of men and women for the worship of almighty God, then it can only be because of one fact: God himself has gathered these tatters of humankind for himself. The life of the people of God, *our* life—is therefore rooted in this: God chooses; God summons; God congregates this congregation and makes them into the people of his pasture and the sheep of his hand.

We find such thoughts very difficult to digest. Partly that's because we are very painfully aware of the sheerly human nature of the Church. This talk about God gathering the Church sounds pretty unrealistic, a fanciful evasion of the fact that the Church is an all-too-human bit of the world. Indeed, it may even sound like a way of cloaking the scandals of the Church by pretending that the Church is a divine society. But the point of talking about God gathering the Church is not to deny that the Church is human, still less to ignore the Church's very evident sinfulness. It is, rather, to say that in all its worldliness, in all its sheer humanness, the Church is a place where God is at work, and at work in God's own way.

What is that way? God's work is not visible in the way that the human aspects of the Church are visible; his work is not tangible like buildings and bishops and pension plans. His work is sacramentally visible: It is visible in the way in which God is visible in baptism and the Lord's Supper. Under the creaturely forms of the sacraments, God is present and active, giving himself to be known and loved. And so with the life of the Church:

Despite everything, this all too fallible institution, with all its muddle and mixed motives and all its shadows, is the place where God is at work, bringing together the people of his pasture and the sheep of his hand.

All this means that at the heart of the Church as the people of God is a divine miracle. That miracle is the miracle of God's grace. What do we mean by that little word "grace?" Grace is God's undeserved, unexpected, unimaginable goodness; grace is God at work to do what no creature can do or ask or imagine. And God's grace in gathering the people of God consists in this: In the midst of human incapacity, in the midst of human enmity or hostility to God, God himself creates a new people to live in fellowship with himself, and above all to gather together to worship him.

God is a God who creates fellowship. All God's works and ways are directed toward making and maintaining the covenant between himself and humankind. God is the creator God, the psalm has already announced to us, and creator not only of the mountains and the hills and valleys and the seas, but also and supremely of a people: He is the Lord our Maker. In the utter perfection of his being, God created humankind. God did not create us out of some need on his part, but out of love. He did not create because he lacked friends, but from the overflowing fullness of his being, God made humankind for fellowship with himself. And the fact that he is our creator and that we are his creatures means this: We are from God, for God, and with God. Because God made us, then we are *from* God; we owe our lives not to ourselves but to God who gave them. Because we are *from* God, we are *for* God. Our true destiny is not something which we make up for ourselves; we are not free to make our lives into what we choose. We are for God; we find out what it means to be human by humbly following the purpose which God has established for us as our creator. And because we are *for* God, then we are *with* God: To be human is to live in fellowship with our creator. From God, for God and with God, we live in fellowship with him.

What's involved in that fellowship with God which is basic to what it means to be a human creature? Fellowship with God means *covenant*. Covenant is the mutual commitment between God and his creatures. In making a covenant with us, God pledges to be our God: to stand by us unfailingly, to watch over us and tend us like as shepherd. And in response to God's pledge, we pledge ourselves to live as God's people: to hold fast to his word and commandment; to direct ourselves in obedience to his guidance; above all, to honor him in our worship. What is the call of every human creature? To live from, and for, and with God, bound to him as he is to us; to turn to God in praise.

But sin brings the covenant fellowship between God and his creatures crashing to the ground. God's creatures turn from God, seeking to be human not in God's way but in a way of their own devising. Refusing God's care and defying God's command, God's creatures seek be their own maker and master, to look after themselves. They repudiate God. They decide that they will not be the people of God's pasture and sheep of his hand, but they will be free, lords of themselves and slaves of no one. And the result of this great act of folly and unrighteousness is *enmity*: hostility between God and his creatures, and hostility between creatures themselves—the shattering of the covenant, the breakdown of the good order of human life, the creature's utter ruin.

When we talk about this reality of human wickedness, we have to remember that we are not just talking about others; we are talking about ourselves. The terrible reality of wickedness is not some sort of pollution which has infected other people but which hasn't got into us. We ourselves are those who have spurned God; we are those who have turned our backs on his covenant; we are those who will not be from God or for God or with God. The devastation of the human race, the destruction of humankind by sin, is our business; we, too, are ruined.

And yet, such is God's mercy that his purpose is not obliterated by the rebellion of his creatures. For how according to the gospel does God deal with our mutiny against himself? Not by putting an end to us; not by banishing us from his presence; not by sweeping us from the face of the earth. No, God deals with our wholesale rejection of him by reconciling us to himself. God comes to our rescue. God looks upon us sinful creatures in all our degradation and defiance, and takes pity on our need, our sheer hopelessness. God matches our hostility by his great work of reconciliation. The fellowship that we have sought to destroy, God maintains. To the covenant that we have renounced, God is unswervingly faithful. Though we may say to God that we will not be his people, he is unshakable in his determination that he will be our God, that he will not allow us to destroy ourselves or to wrest ourselves from his hands. And how does God do this? He does it in the great work of salvation.

In his work of salvation, God grasps hold of human life and binds it to himself; and as he does so, he sets apart for himself a people who will be bound to him, and who will be the sign of his reconciliation of all things to himself. That work of salvation, Scripture tells us, begins with Noah, as God delivers a little body of people from the flood of destruction which sin has unleashed upon the world. It continues in Abraham, who is the father of all those who are to be in covenant with God. It is made firm as Moses stands at the head of God's people on Mount Sinai and seals their covenant with God. It continues through the life of Israel. But it finds its culmination in the life of one man. That one man is Jesus. In him and as him, God deals once and for all with us covenant-breakers. In Jesus, God himself faces the full extent of our hostility, our hatred of himself. Onto him the whole of human rejection is loaded; all our wickedness, all our vanity and folly, all our disobedience—it is all laid on him. He takes it onto himself; and as he does so, he takes it away. He, God himself in the person of his Son, takes away the enmity between us and God and makes peace by the blood of his cross. He reconciles us to God and so restores us to the covenant and to fellowship with God. And the people of that covenant, the new covenant, are the Church—gathered around the presence of the risen Jesus Christ, filled with God's Holy Spirit, made by God into God's own people.

This history of salvation, this work of God to restore the covenant, is the true history of our lives, and so the clue to what we do when we come to church. What's happening when we come to church this morning? It all looks rather ordinary and human: a few clergy, a congregation, a building, a liturgy in 16th-century English prose. But in all these things, the people of God are being gathered; God the Lord of the covenant is at work, speaking, chastising, encouraging, above all summoning us to worship. Here in our gathering this morning—so ordinary, so commonplace—the Lord our Maker is among us and we are being the people of God's pasture and the sheep of his hand.

What is involved in being God's people? A number of things may be said from the psalm about this in closing.

First, *the life of the people of God is the fruit of God's grace.* The people of God are not gathered on the basis of merit, but despite their wickedness and incapacity. The covenant between God and his people is always in a real sense unilateral: God does not cast around for the best possible raw material and mold it into a particularly fine and upstanding holy nation. God takes nothingness and makes it into a Church. God's gathering of the Church is not a reward but an act of absolute mercy. That is why there can be no self-congratulation on the part of the covenant people. We are not here because we ought to be here; we are here because, despite the fact that we ought not to be here, God has pitied us. He has declared himself to be, the psalm says, "our God." But that doesn't mean he is some possession of ours, some household deity there to do what we would like—uphold our cause, ratify our decisions, decorate our way of life. He is always the giver, never the recipient; always the one who is known as supremely exalted and supremely merciful.

Second, *the life of the people of God is life under the Word of God.* "If only you would listen to his voice today!" says the psalm (95:7, NLT). What do we mean by God's Word? We mean, very simply, that God is communicatively present—that God is with us, and that he speaks to us. For fellowship means *presence* and *communication;* life together is a life in which we speak and listen. For the people of God, this means that at the core of fellowship with God is attention to the Word of God. And for Christian people, that means attention to the Word of God as it is announced in Scripture and as it is made visible in the sacraments of the gospel. For in those places—in the Bible, in baptism and the Lord's Supper—the Lord of the Church sets himself before us. In them his voice sounds forth: His law is proclaimed and his promises declared. And the Church is to govern itself by this Word because what it hears there, the psalm says, is *his voice*. Scripture and sacraments are not the Church telling itself something, cheering itself up, or telling itself off. They are the instruments through which the Lord our maker speaks to his people. And so, more than anything, we are to "hearken"—to strain ourselves to listen and to obey the Church's governor.

Third, *the life of the people of God is under God's care.* God's people are God's sheep. But they are not a scattered, helpless flock, exposed to all manner of peril. They are in a deep sense *safe*. They are pastored by him, nurtured, guided and protected by him. By *him*—notice: directly, in person—he cares for his people. He himself, in the person of his Son Jesus Christ, is the great shepherd of the sheep. There are, of course, human under-shepherds, pastors who try to do what they can. But in the end it is his care, God's pastoring of God's people, which is what really matters. Whatever good human pastors may do is simply a pointing to the pastoring of God; their task is merely to testify, to bear witness to the fact that God holds his people in his hand, and will not allow them to perish.

Fourth and supremely, *the life of God's people is life in worship of God.* "Oh come, let us worship and bow down; let us kneel before the Lord, our Maker!" (Psalm 95:6). The repetition there—worship, bow down, kneel—is a way of emphasizing the primacy of this to the life of God's people: The worship of God is not incidental but essential; it is the principal work of those whom God calls into fellowship. This is because in worship we have concentrated for us the fundamental character of the life of the people of God. What's involved in worship? Worship is *thanksgiving*. The *Book of Common Prayer* puts it thus: When we gather for worship, "we assemble and meet together to render thanks for the great benefits we have received at his hands." We gather as those who have been caught up in the great marvel of God's mercy—the mercies of forgiveness, cleansing, God's calling and his daily care.

Worship is *praise*, God's "most worthy praise," which, the *Book of Common Prayer* tells us, we "set forth" in worship: That is, in worship we declare the majesty and goodness of God, describing it lovingly, celebrating it joyfully, echoing back to God the glory which he shows to us. Worship is *hearing*—a hearing of what the *Book of Common Prayer* calls God's "most holy Word." In worship we do not primarily address ourselves to God, but are addressed by God, confronted by his living voice of judgment, pardon, and vocation. And in worship we kneel before God to ask God to do what we cannot do for ourselves: As the *Book of Common Prayer* has it, we "ask those things which are requisite and necessary, as well for the body as the soul." We do not worship out of fullness but out of need, asking the Lord our maker to be just that—our Maker, the one on whom we must rely because he is the one on whom we *can* rely.

Let us remind ourselves of the need to get a true and just vision of our situation. Who are we? We are not just any people, but God's people, those on whom his tender hand has been laid to our great and endless comfort. Where are we? We're not just anywhere; we are in God's pasture, where he cares for us. What is our task? To do the principal work of the human creature, which is to confess God in worship. And so we pray the words of an ancient prayer:

> *O God, the glory of thy saints, who being above all, and through all, and in all, yet dost accept the prayer of the contrite: Grant that we, being hallowed in mind, fervent in spirit, and chaste in body, may offer to thee the pure sacrifice of hearts uplifted in thy praise, and lives devoted to thy service, though Jesus Christ our Lord. Amen.*

CHAPTER 14

OBEYING GOD

Psalm 95:8–11

Do not harden your hearts, as at Meribah,
as on the day at Massah in the wilderness,
when your fathers put me to the test
and put me to the proof, though they had seen my work.
For forty years I loathed that generation
and said, "They are a people who go astray in their heart,
and they have not known my ways."
Therefore I swore in my wrath,
"They shall not enter my rest."

Psalm 95:8–11

WE TURN A THIRD TIME to Psalm 95, thinking especially about the theme of obeying God. We've been trying to read it and hear the psalm as Holy Scripture, following the ancient Anglican tradition of letting Scripture sink into our minds and hearts and wills. In the Anglican *Book of Homilies,* a wonderful collection of Reformation sermons, we read: "Unto a Christian man there can be nothing either more necessary or profitable than the knowledge of Holy Scripture." In line with that, we've been trying in these sermons to read, learn, and inwardly digest the psalm, not simply as a human word but as a divine Word—as the living voice of the living God. Here and now, through this psalm, God addresses us; here and now, in the midst of his assembled people, Jesus Christ in the power of the Spirit confronts us with his Word, judging, absolving, and summoning us to new life, to fresh obedience, and to fellowship with himself.

So far we've seen two things. We've seen, first, how the psalm is an invitation to the praise of God, and we've seen, second, how the psalm speaks of God as our God and of us as God's people, bound together in covenant with God through God's reconciling mercy. But as we move to the third section of the psalm, there is a sudden jolt, a dramatic shift in tone. In the midst of its invitation to celebrate God's presence with his people, the psalm stops us dead in our tracks. And it does so with a simple warning to the people of God as they assemble in worship: "Do not harden not your hearts" (Psalm 95:8a). The psalm began with praise and continued with a reminder of the joyful fact of God's fellowship with his people; suddenly it shifts, to become a stark summons to set aside sin and live in obedience to God. As so often in the psalms, the summons takes the form of a reminder. It takes the listeners back to the wilderness wanderings of the children of

Israel, and in particular it takes them back to the bleak episode of their unbelief in the God who had shown himself their savior by rescuing them from Egypt. Exodus 17:1–7 gives us the story:

> *All the congregation of the people of Israel moved on from the wilderness of Sin by stages, according to the commandment of the Lord, and camped at Rephidim, but there was no water for the people to drink. Therefore the people quarreled with Moses and said, "Give us water to drink." And Moses said to them, "Why do you quarrel with me? Why do you test the Lord?" But the people thirsted there for water, and the people grumbled against Moses and said, "Why did you bring us up out of Egypt, to kill us and our children and our livestock with thirst?" So Moses cried to the Lord, "What shall I do with this people? They are almost ready to stone me." And the Lord said to Moses, "Pass on before the people, taking with you some of the elders of Israel, and take in your hand the staff with which you struck the Nile, and go. Behold, I will stand before you there on the rock at Horeb, and you shall strike the rock, and water shall come out of it, and the people will drink." And Moses did so, in the sight of the elders of Israel. And he called the name of the place Massah and Meribah, because of the quarreling of the people of Israel, and because they tested the Lord by saying, "Is the Lord among us or not?"*

What is the wickedness of the children of Israel here? It is that despite the fact that they have seen God's work—despite the fact that God has brought them out of Egypt with a mighty hand and an outstretched arm, despite the fact that God has shown himself to be the savior—they test God. They want more proof. And so they give voice, as Hebrews puts it, to "an evil, unbelieving heart" (3:12); they abandon faith and test God. They ask the basic question which every unbeliever asks: "Is the Lord among us or not?"

Very soon, of course, they have their answer; the Lord is, indeed, among them. But he is not among them as savior; he is among them as the vengeful Lord of the covenant. The rock of their salvation, the shepherd who feeds and protects his people, is among them in his dreadful majesty as judge. "For forty years I loathed that generation and said, 'They are a people who go astray in their heart, and they have not known my ways.' Therefore I swore in my wrath, 'They shall not enter my rest'" (Psalm 95:10–11).

Now, if we are to hear Holy Scripture aright at this point, we must be very careful. We read of God "loathing" this generation, of God's anger against them. But if we are to make sense of that, we must not fall into the idea that God becomes another God—a God without grace, a God without mercy, a God who is not the redeemer and guardian of his people. God's anger against this wicked generation does not mean that God abandons his covenant. It does not mean that God casts off his people forever, and that his promises are at an end. God's purpose stands fast. His ways will be brought to completion. No sin, no rebellion, no refusal of God, can overthrow the determination of God. If our sins could stand between us and God, then no one would ever have been saved. God has never and will never go back on his avowed purpose that he will be our God and we will be his people of his pasture and the sheep of his hand. God is infinitely greater than all our sins.

Because this is so, then this "loathing" and "anger" of God does not mean that God rejects his people and that he is no longer with them. But it does mean that his presence is the terrifying presence of the judge of all. And that presence purifies by destroying evil. God's anger is not just sheer destructive rage, the kind of thing which afflicts human beings and leads them to smash everything in their sight. God's anger is God setting aside the evil which we sinners have allowed to invade us and take over our lives. It is the fearful energy of his holiness; it is his refusal to let sin have the upper hand. Through his anger, God eradicates sin and evil from the world. And he eradicates evil with a purpose: He eradicates it in order that righteousness and holiness might flourish; he attacks sin to establish the good order of human life. God's anger is not God on the rampage; it is the form of God's love. It is God refusing to let sin triumph; it is God not allowing his people to destroy themselves. God's anger is his faithfulness to the covenant, the purifying power of his love. It doesn't send us to hell; it rescues us from hell.

This episode from the wilderness is not finished business; it is a very present reality. It tells us not just of those people there and then, but of who we are now. We, too, like all human beings, are faced by the same temptation; we, too, are affected by the same evil disease which brings down on us the anger of God. This disease is what the psalm calls hardness of heart.

Hardness of heart, callousness, is what happens when our "hearts"—that is, the core of our lives—become dry and harsh and unyielding. And when our hearts are hard against God, then we will not yield to God. We will not hear his Word. We will not trust ourselves to his saving work. We will not live from him and for him and with him. We will not be his people. Hardness of heart is unbelief and it is disobedience. Such hardness of heart takes many forms. Sometimes it takes the very obvious form of rebellion against God, opposition to God's works and ways, open mutiny against the Lord. But very often it takes more subtle but no less deadly forms. Hardness of heart can be found in us when the life of faith has dried up in some way—when we become careless in our Christian lives, cutting corners, no longer bothering to read Scripture and pray and watch the way we live. It can be found in religious formality, when the form is there but not the substance, when we just go through the motions of the

Christian life, especially the public bits of it, but use religious practice as a cloak for ungodliness.

When our hearts become hard, then we make sure that God doesn't invade us. We banish God from part of our lives—perhaps our work, or our marriage, or our attitude to our neighbors, or even, perhaps, from our Christian faith. We decide that we will allow God to go so far, but not all the way. And when our hearts become hard, then we cease to expect much from God; we allow ourselves to slip into cynicism, and the life of faith withers.

But that's not all. The most ghastly part of this sickness of the soul is that we don't readily admit to ourselves that it's happening; often, indeed, we don't even realize that our hearts have become hard. We can usually convince ourselves that we are not all that bad; we tell ourselves that we just share in the inevitable human shortcomings, and that we can expect no more of ourselves. And in just this way we are entangled in the dreadful falsehood of evil. We are, as Hebrews puts it, "hardened by the deceitfulness of sin" (3:13). We do not know God and we do not know ourselves.

What is God's verdict on us if we are afflicted by this hardness of heart? Two things: We are a people who err in their hearts, and we do not regard God's ways. First, the error lies in the human heart. What's wrong with human life is not some slight, external thing, something which might be corrected by a bit of training or self-discipline. Hardness of heart is a depravity at the core of our beings. "The heart," says Jeremiah, "is deceitful above all things" (17:9). We're not basically good folks who make mistakes and mess up now and again but are essentially sound; we're not just people who occasionally sin. We are sinners. And the basic way in which our sinfulness is expressed is in a refusal to regard God's ways. We shut our eyes and our ears to God. We do not pay heed to his law. We do not look to his works. We do not listen for his Word. We do not want God, and so we turn away.

Such, then, is the psalm's picture of the hardness of heart of the people of God. If we take our understanding of ourselves and our worship not from what we think but from what God declares to us, then we come to realize that our worship involves a conflict between God and our hardness of heart. That conflict between God and sin over who rules the hearts of the worshipers is not the only thing when we get together—of course not. By God's mercy we are able to praise him freely and genuinely, to hear him attentively, to pray to him with humility and trust and hope. But in some measure, all worship and every gathering for the praise of God is infected by our hardness of heart. Each of us in our own way, and all of us together, share in this struggle. We stand in the same line as the children of Israel; their sin, and God's verdict on that sin, is ours too. What must we do?

The psalm's answer is simply this: Listen to his voice. If we would set aside hardness of heart, we must once again become listeners to God. *Where* must we listen? We listen at the place where God speaks, which is Holy Scripture. We listen there because Holy Scripture is the book of the gospel, the good news of God's reconciling work. We listen there because in it the good news of Jesus Christ is proclaimed; there the prophets and apostles testify to the great work of God's mercy, the one who made us for himself, the one who judges and heals us, the one who gives us new life and promises to bring us to share in his glory. And *how* must we listen? We listen with faith. As Hebrews reflects on the sins of God's children in the wilderness, it tells us: "Good news came to us just as to them, but the message they heard did not benefit them, because they were not united by faith with those who listened" (4:2).

What is faith? Faith is the very opposite of hardness of heart. Where hardness of heart is stubborn and intractable, faith yields to God. It does not test; it does not seek to prove; it does not scrutinize God to check whether he is as reliable as he claims. Faith takes God at his word; very simply, it listens to his voice. *With whom* must we listen? We listen with the people of God, with those to whom we are bound in fellowship. We cannot guard our hearts on our own, for we are callous and deceive ourselves. We need others to minister God's Word to us. And so as Hebrews puts it: "Exhort one another every day ... that none of you may be hardened by the deceitfulness of sin" (3:13). And last, *when* must we listen? Today—for every day is God's today, the day of judgment and grace, the day when he speaks his word of mercy and when we must listen to him.

These are solemn matters. If we are spiritual people, we may easily be discouraged by what is said to us—we may easily feel that our case is hopeless, and that we will never climb out of our sins. For so often it seems to us that, try as we might, we cannot help ourselves: We cannot listen well, we cannot greet God's Word with faith, we cannot soften our hard hearts. Of course we can't. We can no more improve our spiritual lives than we can raise ourselves from the dead. But what we cannot do, God can and will do. God has not left matters in our hands; we are in the hands of Jesus Christ. And he, Jesus Christ, is Lord of all things—*all* things, including our hearts, our wills, our desires, our hopes. He takes hold of us; he does for us what we cannot do for ourselves. By his Spirit he brings new life. And so, if today we would hear his voice and set aside all the sins which cling to us, we must pray this prayer:

> *O Lord our God, who didst send thy Holy Spirit to abide with thy Church forever: renew the same Spirit within us, that our hearts may be cleansed from evil, and that faith, hope and love may abound in our lives; to the glory of Jesus Christ our Savior. Amen.*

CHAPTER 15

THE HEARING CHURCH

Revelation 3:13, 14

He who has an ear, let him hear what the Spirit says to the churches. ... "The words of the Amen, the faithful and true witness, the beginning of God's creation."

Revelation 3:13, 14

One of the most startling things about the book of Revelation is that it is shot through with a conviction that Jesus Christ *speaks*. The Apocalypse as a whole is filled with voices: shouts of praise and terror; laments; words of warning, condemnation, and promise: almost the whole range of human speech. Yet over and above all the other voices, there is the one great speaker, the first and the last, the one from whose mouth there issues a sharp two-edged sword. And that speaker is Jesus himself. He is the living one; and as he lives he also speaks. His aliveness is eloquent. He presides over the world's history, he draws all things to their goal, he completes the destruction of all that stands opposed to the purposes of God. And as he does so, he lifts up his voice and speaks to the world in a way which is inescapably real and utterly commanding. He is not mute or absent or inert. On the contrary, he is the faithful and true witness, and his testimony, his Word, intercepts and judges and makes all things new.

This vivid sense that the risen Jesus is speaker astonishes or perplexes us. Where we are tempted to be embarrassed by its fervor, the Apocalypse is not at all embarrassed to talk in very direct terms of the vocal presence of Jesus. Our perplexity, of course, is rooted in the fact that we find ourselves in a culture which functionally and theoretically has ceased to expect divine speech. The conviction on which the Apocalypse is based—that God in Christ is a speaker, and that if we are to interpret human history we have to listen to the voice of God—is to all intents and purposes not an operative one for us. We work on the assumption that God is silent. If true words are to be spoken, we ourselves have to say them.

Figuring out why we work on that assumption is of course an enormously complex business, and getting beyond that assumption is even more difficult for us. How are we to move beyond it? How may we begin to think of the world as the kind of place where God is to be heard? If we are somehow to get back into the world so strikingly set before us in the Apocalypse, it cannot be by theory. That is, the problem we find ourselves in is not something that can be solved by just inventing clever arguments to reassure ourselves of the possibility that God speaks. Much more is it a matter of learning again a certain kind of practice. It's a matter of relearning the habits of mind and soul in which listening for the voice of the risen Christ is the natural and obvious way of encountering the truth of our lives. Above all, it is a matter of rediscovering what it means to be a community of the Word of God.

The community of the Word of God is the community that is brought into being and sustained by the fact that Jesus Christ speaks. The Word that constitutes the community and governs its life is the good news, the message of salvation at whose center lie the ministry and death and resurrection of Jesus Christ and the hope of his return. Those events are set before us in highly dramatic terms in the Apocalypse as the destruction of sin and death and the vindication of the saints; as such they are a Word. That is, they aren't just neutral, flat facts that we can consider from afar, as if they were not really our concern, as if they did not really impinge on us. On the contrary, they address us. As Word they accost us, they come to us as divine communication, they seek us out and set themselves in our midst, for Jesus Christ himself is the prophetic voice of his own saving work. And so the Christian community is, at heart, that community which is judged, acquitted, shaken, consoled, and encouraged by the fact that the Spirit—the risen Christ present before us—speaks to the churches. To be the Church is to be spoken to by Jesus in the Spirit. To be faithful is to "keep his word." To be alive and alert is to hear what the Spirit has to say.

The primary activity of the community of the Word, therefore, is a rather odd sort of activity: the passive activity of hearing. Only once spoken to does the Church itself speak. In the Anglican tradition—seemingly a million miles away from these bizarre charismatic communities of the apocalypse—the primacy of hearing the words of the living Jesus in the Spirit is expressed as the primacy in church of the reading of Holy Scripture. It's the lectern which is the primary home of the Word of God in church, not the pulpit. It's Scripture read, not Scripture proclaimed, which is the first great act of speech in church. To be the Church, to be the community of Jesus Christ which is concerned with the gospel, is first and foremost to listen, to strain our attention toward that Word which God himself, present among us as the risen and ascended Christ in the power of the Holy Spirit, now addresses to us in the text of Holy Scripture. Here, as always, the fundamental rule: I heard, and so I speak.

But more needs to be said, and it is this. Our hearing of the Word of the living Christ is *threatened*. In the letters to the seven churches in these early chapters of the apocalypse, the living Jesus speaks his Word to communities whose hearing has in some sense failed—for hearing may go wrong. And the reason for this is that hearing takes place in the midst of the same basic struggle which is true of all reality, the struggle of God against sin. No less than anything else in the life of the community of Jesus Christ, its listening partakes of the dynamic of resistance to God. We refuse to hear. We oppose the Word of God. What forms does this opposition take? There are, it seems, two very basic modes of this resistance to or repudiation of the Word.

The first, the most dramatic and scandalous form, is outright opposition to or denial of the Word. At its heart this is a resistance to God which will not bear the content of what it is that the gospel says to us, and which expresses that resistance not by being politely deaf, but by pushing the Word away, by revolt, a kind of adamant refusal to be spoken to in this manner. The final exhortation in both sections of our reading—"He who has an ear, let him hear" (Revelation 3:13)—drives the point home: We're involved in a collision between the voice of God and our stubbornness and repudiation. In our easy-going ways as tolerant moderns, we tend not to see the Christian life in quite these terms. What earlier generations of Christians might have seen as opposition to the Word of God we sometimes regard as a sort of benign open-mindedness. But it's worth saying that there is all the difference in the world between, on the one hand, a genuine diversity of ways of hearing and, on the other hand, resistance to the gospel—and that sometimes what we think of as legitimate diversity may just be a form of opposition to God. The second form repudiation of the Word is not a matter of revolting against the Word but of converting it into something much more amenable to our unregenerate tastes. Rather than being dismissed, the Word is reinvented. But such hearing is no hearing at all. It doesn't listen to God, but talks to itself, and what it says to itself sounds pretty good. Yet however pleasing it may be, such hearing is a death-blow, above all because it cuts off the Church from that genuine attention in which alone is its source of life. Once the Word is not a judge but a pacifier, then truth has been traded away. The Church's hearing is cushioned; it doesn't hit the reality of the gospel like a brick wall.

So the Church's hearing is threatened by the primary form of human sin, which is to cease to listen to God and to substitute or supplement what God says with something that God does not say. What remedy is there for the situation? How may the Church's hearing be secured? Very simply, the remedy is that the Church has to take the law of its own existence with absolute seriousness. It's founded by God to be a community that hears the Word of God, and so it must hear that Word. When hearing is threatened, in other words, the only thing to do is to listen properly. There is no technique that the Church can perform here, no infallible method that will guarantee that once and for all it will get it right. Renewal is nothing other than a matter of the Church being the Church, fulfilling its call, holding fast to its commission. But that being said, two further points may be established.

First, hearing the Word of the gospel demands a certain definiteness on the part of the Christian community. It demands, that is, that the Church be *this* community, the community of Jesus Christ, the community that keeps his Word and does not deny his name. Hearing his Word requires that the Church have a certain clarity of profile, a clear shape. The Christian community will function well when it is much absorbed by listening to its Scripture, seeking the voice of God there, without worrying too much about other voices to which it might attend. There has to be a certain focused intensity in the Church's listening: Here, not there, we are to expect God's address of us, and so here, not there, is where we will wait.

Second, and last, the Church's hearing is a gift of the Holy Spirit. We are sinners; we do not know how to hear. Right hearing is not within the range of our competence. It's given to us, given by the activity of God's Spirit in which God opens the ears of the deaf, making it possible for us to become true hearers of God's Word. If we hear because the Spirit makes it possible for us to do so, then at the heart of the life of the Church, and at the heart of its listening to the Bible, will be prayer—prayer for the coming of God's Spirit, prayer in which the Spirit is invoked because he alone establishes us in the Word. What is the real mark of the Church of Jesus Christ? It's that in everything we do—believing, celebrating, praising, interceding, proclaiming, suffering, listening—we make one prayer: *Come, Holy Spirit.*

And so we pray:

O heavenly Father, in whom is the fullness of light and wisdom, enlighten our minds by thy Holy Spirit, and give us grace to receive thy Word with reverence and humility, without which no one can understand and speak thy truth; for the sake of Jesus Christ, our Lord. Amen.

Part IV

LIVING BY PROMISES

CHAPTER 16

GOD'S SUSTAINING PRESENCE

Psalm 121

I lift up my eyes to the hills.
From where does my help come?
My help comes from the Lord,
who made heaven and earth.

He will not let your foot be moved;
he who keeps you will not slumber.
Behold, he who keeps Israel
will neither slumber nor sleep.

The Lord is your keeper;
the Lord is your shade on your right hand.
The sun shall not strike you by day,
nor the moon by night.

The Lord will keep you from all evil;
he will keep your life.
The Lord will keep
your going out and your coming in
from this time forth and forevermore.

Psalm 121

THE THEME OF PSALM 121 is a question which presses daily upon the people of God: "From where does my help come?" (121:1). That is: Who keeps God's people? Who maintains their life? Who is it that they must turn to in distress? In the midst of the vexation and the guilt which press in on God's people, in whose name is their help to be found? And the answer that the psalm gives to those questions is simple and direct and yet gives us enough for a lifetime of thought and prayer: "My help comes from the Lord" (121:2). What are we to make of the question and its answer?

First, we will not make much sense of what the psalm has to say unless we can see that the question "From where does my help come?" is a real and persistent question for people of God—for these people of God in the psalm, and for us, the company of Jesus Christ. God's people are always in some measure distressed. They need help. It is a basic part of the experience of God's people that their lives are characterized by affliction. And that affliction is not some abnormal or occasional state of affairs, a temporary visitor. Distress, affliction, and neediness are permanent and basic characteristics of the life of God's people; they are built into the condition in which they exist. This distress takes many forms. But behind the question which the psalm asks, there seem to be two particular kinds of adversity which beset God's people, both of which we may readily recognize as our own.

One kind of adversity is weariness. Weariness is the distress which comes when we realize that our resources are simply not up to what we have to do. Whether on our own or in our common life, we are utterly overwhelmed by the task which faces us. As the community of Jesus Christ, we have to carve out a way of living in a society which does not care a fig for the

Christian gospel, which almost never thinks of the Church—or, if it does think of the Church, thinks of it as a joke, or a handy source of moral maxims or wedding venues. As individual believers, we find that serious discipleship, making the gospel and the Christian confession our own, in some measure makes us strangers to our neighbors. There's so much to which we have to say "No," so much which offends or wounds or disaffects us. For both the Christian community and the individual believer, the long-term effect of this kind of estrangement can be a deep exhaustion; if we are to hold on to our confession, if we are to swim against the tide and not just drift with it, we will become deeply drained. And so we must ask: Who will keep us? Who will hold our lives when we can do so ourselves no longer?

A second kind of adversity is directionlessness. There is a spiritual unsteadiness which comes from feeling that the ground is moving beneath our feet. This kind of adversity often besets the Church as an institution. One common symptom of it is church leaders making public their uncertainties about what the Church is called to be or whether the gospel is really true; it takes the form of a crisis of confidence in the viability of the Church's life of faith. The effect is that the mission of the Church quickly becomes incoherent and aimless, grasping at all sorts of things to try and give the impression that we know who we are and what we are supposed to be about; but none of this can hide the fact that at heart what's being expressed is a heavy sense of aimlessness. And so, again, we have to ask: Who will preserve our going out and our coming in (121:8)? Who will direct us in our ways?

Thus the psalm faces us with our weariness, and with our incapacity to set a bearing and direct ourselves on the right path. Now, in this situation of distress out of which the psalm comes, we must avoid two false answers to the question of where our help is to be found. We must not despair; and we must not look to any sources of assistance but to God alone. We must avoid despair, because despair is unbelief. To despair of our situation, however taxing, however threatening, is to say that God has no help for us, that God himself has no resources with which to sustain us, and that therefore there is no one to keep us and preserve us. But we may not escape from the anguish of our confession by denying our confession. We must learn that, for the people of God, surrendering is simply not an option. And, moreover, we must avoid looking to other sources of assistance.

One of the most common forms of our human perversity is the inconstancy in which we look around to any number of places for help, but never direct ourselves to the one place where help can really be found. Need doesn't always drive us into the arms of God. Often enough it does the opposite: It becomes yet another occasion for running away from the truth, for refusing that painful healing in which alone is our well-being. Even our need becomes an opportunity for sin. We are in need, serious need; and part of our vexation is that we struggle against our need. It's not just that we need help; it's that we can't accept that the help we need is in God alone.

In just this jeopardy and peril God meets us. In his mercy, God overrules our hopelessness and perversity, and sets before us the single fact that is at the core of the psalm's confession: Our help comes from God. There is help for God's people; it really does come; and it comes from God alone. What more may we learn of this from the psalm?

First, and basically, our help comes from the Lord alone. He will not suffer us to be moved; he will keep Israel; he is our keeper and defence; he will keep our soul. The help of the people of God in affliction is in God alone. How will we survive? Not because of any strength or cleverness or virtue of our own; not because we can somehow find in ourselves or in our culture the resources to win through; above all, not because we can be busy about the enterprise of self-preservation. We will survive because and only because of who God is and what God does. And so, who is this God who is our help and preserver? And what does he do in this matter of our need?

He is maker of heaven and earth, and therefore our maker, the one to whom we owe our very being (121:2). In making this confession of the God who comes to our help, we are confessing two things of supreme goodness and power to encourage. We are confessing that the Lord who is our helper is almighty. He is the one who brings life out of nothing; he is the Lord, the giver of life. And that means that he is not powerless against our afflictions in the way that we are. He does not suffer from our distresses, he is not overwhelmed by what masters us. He is the Lord, the one whose power is infinite. And because he is such, and because he turns to us in our need and helps us, we are indeed helped. We do not stand isolated, but we are in the hands of almighty God. And because we confess that God is creator, we also confess that he is the governor of all things. The God of creation is also the God of providence. What God makes, God governs; God stands in constant and faithful and loving relation to what he has made. The creation is not made and then released from his hand to go wherever it will. It is held by him. It is preserved by him. With unfathomable gentleness and secrecy God guides all things to their true end. He appoints his creation for glory, and under his governance all things will be glorified.

Who does this? God himself does it. The Lord himself is thy keeper, the psalmist confesses. That is, God the Lord, creator of all things and governor of all things, himself preserves and keeps us. The psalm's confession is unthinkable without a sense that God is himself active in relation to what he has made. For the Christian confession, this active relation, this sustaining presence of God, is the presence of Jesus Christ and the Holy Spirit. Because Jesus Christ is alive and enthroned and rules over all things, and because in the power, the supreme power, of the Holy Spirit Jesus Christ is with us and among us and in us, then we may confess that the Lord himself is our keeper. We confess that the Lord is our keeper because Jesus Christ is present; because through his Spirit our lives are caught up into his purposes; because in our affliction and distress we are not left without his aid. Above all, we confess that the Lord himself is our keeper because of the promise of God: I will not leave you comfortless. That's why the Church of Jesus Christ, faced with weariness and lack of direction, can confess: "The Lord will keep you from all evil; he will keep your life" (121:7).

What then of the practical importance of this confession? How will it shape us as we live for God? Two things.

First, we must pray for the grace of composure. There's a calmness, a quiet and yet very real confidence in the psalm. God does not sleep through the misery of the world; God will shade us in the heats of the day; God will watch us as we journey; God will keep us. It's simple enough. But to get to those affirmations, we have to climb over a lot of rubble inside ourselves. We have to learn what is extraordinarily hard for us to learn: not to listen to our fears; not to be tossed around by whatever comes across our path; not to give credence to the lies that God has fallen asleep or just given up protecting us. Those things take a lifetime to learn for most of us, because learning them involves overcoming some of our most basic drives and desires and foolishness. But it's only as we learn those things that we begin to live with a measure of Christian composure. Christian composure is a very particular thing, however. It's an equanimity that is given to us, which we don't make up from our own resources. It's given to us as we make our confession of the lordship of God, as we learn how to praise God, how to trust the gospel, how to see all things in the light of God's mercy, how to keep our hearts by God's promises.

Second, we must come to see where we truly are. We're in the hands of God. We're in his presence. More than anything else, we've been set in fellowship with him, for he is our God and we are his people, and so we are not left to our own devices. More than anything else, the Church of Jesus Christ and the individual members of that Church need to set their hearts on reality. And reality is this: God is at our right hand. God is our preserver. The God who made heaven and earth comes to our assistance. St. Augustine says this:

> Choose for yourself Him, who will neither sleep nor slumber, and your foot shall not be moved. God is never asleep: if you wish to have a keeper who never sleeps, choose God for your keeper.

But St. Augustine knew very well that we can choose God only because God has chosen us, has destined us to be those who are kept and preserved by him, for his glory and our endless comfort. Amen.

CHAPTER 17

THE CALL TO REMEMBRANCE

Psalm 78:1–20

Give ear, O my people,
to my teaching;
incline your ears
to the words of my mouth!
I will open my mouth in a parable;
I will utter dark sayings
from of old,
things that we have heard
and known,
that our fathers have told us.
We will not hide them
from their children,
but tell to the coming generation
the glorious deeds of the LORD*,*
and his might,
and the wonders that he has done.

He established a testimony in Jacob
and appointed a law in Israel,
which he commanded our fathers
to teach to their children,
that the next generation
might know them,
the children yet unborn,
and arise and tell them
to their children,
so that they should set their hope
in God
and not forget the works of God,
but keep his commandments;
and that they should not be
like their fathers,
a stubborn and rebellious
generation,
a generation whose heart
was not steadfast,
whose spirit was not faithful
to God.
The Ephraimites, armed
with the bow,
turned back on the day of battle.
They did not keep God's covenant,
but refused to walk
according to his law.
They forgot his works
and the wonders that he
had shown them.
In the sight of their fathers
he performed wonders
in the land of Egypt,
in the fields of Zoan.
He divided the sea and let them
pass through it,
and made the waters stand
like a heap.
In the daytime he led them
with a cloud,
and all the night with a fiery light.
He split rocks in the wilderness
and gave them drink abundantly
as from the deep.
He made streams come out
of the rock
and caused waters to flow down
like rivers.
Yet they sinned still more
against him,
rebelling against the Most High
in the desert.
They tested God in their heart
by demanding the food
they craved.
They spoke against God, saying,
"Can God spread a table
in the wilderness?
He struck the rock so that
water gushed out
and streams overflowed.
Can he also give bread
or provide meat for his people?"

Psalm 78:1–20

THE PSALM ON WHICH WE ARE focusing our thoughts is a psalm of remembrance. It's a psalm which puts memory to work in the life of obedience to God and the gospel. What is memory? Memory is that part of the mystery of human life through which the past can still be present to us—through which what we have been and what we have done remains part of us now, so that through memory we can re-present the past to ourselves, make it part of our present now. It would be hard to over-estimate the importance of memory in the biblical tradition, especially in the Psalter. For Scripture, memory is a critical faculty in the life of the people of God, for the simple reason that God is the God of covenant. God is the God who enters into covenant with a people; and God's great acts of salvation in the past are the basis both of present commands and future promises. Because God has done this, because God has acted thus and shown himself to be this one, then we are now faced with a command to live in a certain way, and a hope that we will have a certain future—and therefore we must remember.

The remembering which is required of us is not, of course, some sort of idle entertainment of the past, unfocussed reverie in which we let the past float before our eyes and then slip out of consciousness. Memory is the urgent business of setting before our eyes God's great act of delivering us from death and giving us a share in his life. Memory, remembering the past, governs our present and our future. It is through remembering that our identity now is set out—what we are now is the people who have been called into being by God's mighty acts of deliverance. So to know who we are, we must remember. It is through remembering that our present life is to be assessed. How should we act in the present? We should act as those who look back to these mighty acts and, as it were, stand beneath them, acknowledging them as a summons to a distinctive life of obedience to God's grace. And it is through remembering that our future is secured. What we will be is to be shaped by our recalling of the deeds of God, and our trusting ourselves to them as promises of his future faithfulness. As he has been, he forever will be.

Memory is thus a basic part of what it means to be a covenant people. It's an intrinsic aspect of understanding ourselves as having a life in relation to God, a life in which God elects and calls and sanctifies a people for himself, and in which God calls us to a faithfulness which matches his own faithfulness. Memory is crucial because in it we grasp hold of the covenant character of our relation to the God of grace.

Such is the background to the psalm. Its context, more likely than not, is some kind of public celebration to renew the covenant in the life of Israel, some public point in Israel's life in which the covenant is set before the people in a fresh and vivid way as both indicative and imperative—as an announcement of salvation and a call to obedience. The opening verses of the psalm are in very characteristic Wisdom-literature style, a bit like the kind of thing at the beginning of Proverbs. It addresses the hearers of the psalm, assembled to listen again to the testimony and the law, setting two things before them: the reality of God's mighty works, and the reality of human rebellion. And on that basis it calls for a fresh remembrance of God's salvation and a fresh commitment to faithfulness to God. The psalm aims to set before its hearers a great recital of the ways and works of God which will seize hold of the life of people of God, counter their drift away from the covenant and ensure that their obedience to God's law is fulfilled. It is written, as it says, "so that they should set their hope in God and not forget the works of God, but keep his commandments" (78:7).

One further thing about the context of this psalm is crucial, however, to hearing what it has to say to us. The call to remembrance, the call to renewal of life in covenant faithfulness, is a call which is issued in the midst of human disobedience. It is God's people as *sinners* who are here accosted by God's call. That call is not one which is eagerly anticipated, gladly heard and greeted with delight. It is resisted. It is spurned. It is rejected. Why? Because is it a call to a kind of remembering which faces us with the bleakness of our human failure to be the people whom God has appointed us to be. The remembering which the psalm is looking to is not therefore just some happy natural capacity. Remembering God and God's mighty acts of salvation are not something we can do just by turning our minds in the right direction. The remembering for which the psalm calls is painful, disturbing and dangerous; it is something which we have almost to be forced to do. Hence the imperious summons in verse 1 of the psalm: Listen! Incline your ears! Do not turn away! Do not be deaf to the word, the parable or prophecy, which is addressed to you. Let God's Word speak to you with power (78:1).

Remembering means being exposed to judgment. It means facing the truth from which we ordinarily hide. The judgment happens because remembering exposes the yawning gulf between God's great acts of faithfulness and our sheer human infidelity. Remembering shows us the inescapable truth about God and about ourselves.

Who is the God whom we encounter in remembrance? He is the God of Exodus. He is the God who for no other reason than the sheer abundance of his mercy and love took Israel to be his own people, his special possession. He is the one who elected that there should be a human object of his creative love. He is the one who despite all the odds established this people by setting them free from their masters and gave them the most precious freedom imaginable—the freedom to obey the Lord God himself. He is the one before whom the sea divided and the rocks were split. He is the one who led and fed his people in the wilderness. And so, quite simply, he is the God of salvation, the one who makes the impossible to be possible, who brings into being the things that are not.

And who are we in this encounter? What does it mean to encounter ourselves in remembrance of the covenant of God? In answer to this question, the psalm is devastating and complete in its judgment. Here at least the Scripture does not set before us a picture of human life as ambiguous, partly good and partly bad, a nuanced mixture of shades. It states before us our irrevocable condemnation. It sums us up in three simple words: "Yet they sinned" (78:17). In what does that sin consist? It is a failure to keep God's covenant, a failure to answer God's faithful love of us with our echoing love of God. The forms of that failure, the psalm tells us, are manifold: forgetting the works of God, stubbornness and rebellion, refusing to walk according to God's law, rebellion against the Most High. But all of these forms are manifestations of the same thing: They are all ways of living without remembrance of the covenant, ways of living as if God were not the God of the covenant and we were not called to be his people, as if somehow we could forget that we are elected and appointed by this God. And so, the psalm tells us:

> *They tested God in their heart*
> *by demanding the food they craved.*
> *They spoke against God, saying,*
> *"Can God spread a table in the wilderness?*
> *He struck the rock so that water gushed out*
> *and streams overflowed.*
> *Can he also give bread*
> *or provide meat for his people?"*
> *(Psalm 78:18–20)*

They tested God. That is, they entertained the thought that maybe God is not the God that he has shown himself to be; they stood apart from God; they took a look at him and wondered if he could possibly match up to their needs and expectations. And they did all this "in their heart" (78:18). They fell into the fatal trap of thinking that the secret recesses within each of us are somehow hidden from God—that inside each of us there is some deep place where we can entertain any thoughts or possibilities that we choose and the Lord will not see or know. To do this, to test God in the heart, is to break covenant faith. It is to walk away from the covenant—to walk away from that natural and unreflective and immediate life with God, and to follow the lie that we can be ourselves without God.

So, we have a psalm of remembrance—above all, about remembrance of the fact that the life of the people of God is caught up within the great drama of obedience and disobedience, of grace versus ingratitude, of divine fidelity versus human faithlessness. What does it mean for us now to hear this as Holy Scripture? In particular, what does it mean for the life of common prayer which is the core of our life as God's people?

Remembrance is never far from the center of public prayer. Part of what both Scripture and sacrament do to us is lay before us a permanent reminder of the gospel and its judgment. They are points at which we gather, perhaps unwillingly, perhaps fearfully, to hear the Word which breaks us open and exposes us to the reality which we would rather live without and push into forgetfulness. What do we remember when we gather thus to pray?

We remember that we are sinners. To face God in prayer, public or private, is to face the one whom we cannot face, from whom we must avert our eyes. We cannot face God because, though we are marked out as God's chosen people, we would rather not bear that mark in our lives. We would rather not be disturbed by God; we would rather be left in peace. Gathering together to pray ensures that this kind of false peace cannot be ours. And so to pray is to confess—to acknowledge, to say to ourselves and to others and to God—the truth which we would rather hide, the truth that we are covenant-breakers.

But we remember also that we are the people whom the Lord Jesus feeds. In the wilderness, the psalm reminds us, God cleaved the rock to give his people drink, and sent food to satisfy their hunger. And in the gospel we hear how Jesus, faced with the sheer need of the multitude who gathered around him, took the loaves and fish and gave thanks and broke them and distributed them, and they were all satisfied. So for us: Jesus is among us, our host at his table. He takes bread, and breaks it and offers it to us; he takes wine and gives it to us to drink. And why? So that we will remember. He gives us these tokens so that we may lodge in our memories and hearts and minds and wills that once for all on that Friday afternoon his body was broken so that we might be healed. In that dying, the covenant is remade, and we are set free to praise him and to serve him among his people.

CHAPTER 18

THE NATURE OF FAITH

Hebrews 11:1

Now faith is the assurance of things hoped for, the conviction of things not seen.

Hebrews 11:1

Often when we think and talk about faith, we fall into a trap. The trap is that of thinking of faith as some sort of special power or faculty that we have, or at least that we ought to have. We think of faith as a sort of natural talent, a bit like being good at arithmetic or having a flair for gardening—again, some power or capacity we have or would like to possess. Very often thinking in this way about faith is bound up with a sense of frustration about ourselves, a sense that to some extent we are deficient Christians because we don't seem to have much of a talent for faith. "If only we had more faith," we chastise ourselves; if only we had a great measure of this mysterious power which would somehow make the Christian life more real and lift us out of our doubts and confusions.

The problem with thinking along these lines is that it begins in the wrong place. It begins with us: our attitudes, our emotions, our inner lives. And in this it tends to reinforce the false idea that sorting out how to live a life of faith is basically a matter of figuring ourselves out. It can encourage us in the idea that getting faith right means cultivating some attitude, putting our inner lives on some sort of disciplined regime. And the result of that is that we're disoriented from the start. The basic rule for thinking about faith is this: What matters about faith is not us, but the object of faith. Faith isn't primarily a power or capacity in me; it isn't first and foremost an attitude which I adopt; indeed, it's not first of all something which I do. Faith is objective—that is, faith is wholly turned outward to the object of faith. In a real sense, it's not faith itself but that toward which faith is turned that is critically important in getting our thinking straight. What matters about faith is therefore not us but God, the object of faith.

But here perhaps faith still seems a very disconcerting business. For what is this object of faith? Hebrews 11 tell us that it's "things hoped for" and "things not seen." The object of faith, that is, is frustratingly absent. Faith's object is something for which we hope—things that are not here. Faith's object is invisible. What faith is about, what faith turns toward, isn't available in a straightforward way. It's not present to us unambiguously like tables and chairs and people and all the other things that make up the world. Faith's object is simply not something which we can handle; it's not a bit of the secure, manageable world. It's on the other side of the world, beyond the horizon, beyond our sight and our touch, in one sense even beyond our knowledge. In faith we do business with God. Yet even in doing business with God we never get to a point where we see and know God directly. There's no immediate vision; there's no point, not even in faith itself, at which the barrier between us and God is dismantled and we are face to face with God. What there is now—all there is now—is hope, not sight.

Because of this, faith is contested. It's contested by those who don't share our faith, and we ourselves contest it. We often feel dismayed by the fact that what we have believed in is so frustratingly intangible, invisible, apparently so far out of our reach. So often it seems as if faith is hanging in mid-air, insecure, ungrounded, utterly perilous and exposed. Now, because faith seems suspended in nothingness, we often try to replace it with something else. We look for tangible reassurances. Rather than hope, we want possession; rather than things glimpsed in the half-light of faith (1 Corinthians 13:12), we want something we can see clearly and unambiguously. And so we build up a great array of tangible substitutes for the God whom we encounter in faith. Sometimes we place a great deal of weight on arguments and ideas, looking to them to provide some sort of reliable, uncontested ground for faith. At other times, we look to experiences of God; very often we're tempted to think that experience will give us a sort of direct route to God which will shortcut all the ambiguities and hesitations of the life of faith.

Of course arguments and experiences have their place, but they are not gods. They may not substitute for the God who is known in faith. And the trouble with these tangible reassurances is that they threaten to do just that: They are a flight from faith. They seem, of course, to be quite the opposite—a way of confirming faith, a way of proving to ourselves that what we trust in faith really is real and trustworthy. But in fact they're a spurning of God; they're a refusal to have God on God's terms. They turn their backs on the way in which God encounters us and instead look for something different, something better, something without the apparent fragility and vulnerability of faith. They don't want to see something from afar; they want to see it clearly, here and now. They don't want to live in the land of promise; they want to arrive, to be in the city.

To want those things is enmity with God. It's to want God on our terms, and therefore not to want God. Or, we might say, it's to want a different god from the God who really encounters us. It's to replace God with an idol, and so to commit the great sin of religion. Religion is sin when it makes God into something which we can handle. Whether we handle God through graven images or theological ideas or liturgy and music or ecstatic experience doesn't really matter. It's all idolatry, all a flight from the city which God builds, all a way of saying that God as God isn't good enough, and that if God is to be worth trusting he'll have to conform to our expectations and needs. None of us is exempt; all of us have to realize that religion always carries with it the danger that we will make God into the likeness of something on earth, and in doing so we will lose faith, and lose God.

What are we to say about our capacity for idolatry, our ability to destroy faith by making it something tangible? One temptation is to go to the other extreme—that is, the temptation is to say that, because the object of faith isn't tangible and visible, then faith is in fact pure risk, a leap into nothingness, an utterly empty space. But Hebrews does not allow us to think in such terms. Faith, it tells us, isn't sheer abandonment of ourselves to nothing; it is conviction and hope. Faith isn't simple blindness; it's a real seeing of things not seen. But that of which we have a conviction, that in which we hope and which we see, has a special character. The object of faith is real to us in a special way. Faith is not simple seeing, but nor is it sheer blindness. Faith is that kind of seeing which corresponds to the way in which God is visible; it's that kind of knowing which corresponds to the way in which God gives himself to be known. Faith is the way in which we meet and respond to the God who sets himself before us, to be known and seen as who he truly is.

Because of this, there are a couple of things which need to be said about faith if we are to think about it in the right way, especially if we are to deal with the nagging fear we often have that faith is a pretty defenseless and insecure business.

First, faith is grounded in God's promises. Hebrews 11 gives us a long recital of the heroes of faith from the Old Testament—Noah, Abraham, Sarah, and all the rest. The point of appealing to these witnesses is that they all lived and acted out their lives on the basis of the promises of God. They took God at his word; they acted on the basis of what God said. They heard, surrendered, and obeyed. They therefore abandoned the desire for tangible certainty, because they came to see that desire for that kind of certainty in the end prevented them from knowing God. But they also knew that because faith is rooted in God's promise it entails assurance and conviction. One promise of God is worth more than all the proof in the world. Why? Because it's a promise from God. A proof is just what I come up with, or what some other authority comes up with. It bears only the authority of a creature and a sinner. But a promise comes to me with the competence and purity and trustworthiness of God. And so faith has its certainty, which is a certainty rooted in God, and which enables us by faith to sojourn in the land of promise.

Second, therefore, faith grounded in God's promises is a matter of hope. Hope in the Christian sense isn't blind. It's not unfocused longing or fantasizing about what might be. Hope, like faith, has an object, it has a basis. But the object and basis of hope, like the object and basis of faith, isn't available in a straightforward way. It's something which has been declared to us by God, and which can be glimpsed, not here and now, but on the horizon, at the very edge of our vision. Like Abraham's city, it's something seen and greeted from afar (11:8–10, 13–16). Hope isn't defeated by this, because it's grounded in God's Word, in God's declaration of his promise. Faith and hope in God are not mere credulity. They're sustained and supported by God. And that means they're sustained and supported by the fact that God is communicative, eloquent. God is not silent; God says, as Isaiah puts it, "Incline your ear, and come to me; hear, that your soul may live" (Isaiah 55:3).

Faith is therefore a matter of taking God at God's word. Abraham showed faith because he was called and, having been called, obeyed (Hebrews 11:8). What calls us, what we are to obey, is *God's* Word, of course—not some human word, or some human version of God's Word. And because it's God's Word, it's a Word which we have as we have God: as a gift, not as a possession. The Word speaks of what we do not see and what we do not have. But because it's God's Word which calls, it brings assurance and conviction—the knowledge that, with Abraham, God himself is our inheritance (Genesis 15:1; Psalm 73:26).

What's the practical consequence of all this? Faith is the inescapable way in which we live our lives now in relation to God. We cannot get beyond it; there are, again, no other terms on which we can have God. Faced with this fact, we can react one of two ways. We can rail against it, or we can accept it as part of our condition. All of us at some point or another certainly rail against faith: Why can't God be plain, obvious, here and now? The answer, of course, is because God is God. That doesn't stop us wanting what we can't have, but God is not to be had in that way. To accept it, on the other hand, is simply to realize that we are who we are, God is who God is, and there matters must rest. We can no more get beyond faith than we can get beyond time and space and our bodies. We must learn, like Abraham, how to sojourn "in the land of promise, as in a foreign land" (Hebrews 11:9).

How do we do that? We do it, first, by learning how to live with a certain uprootedness, however hard that may be. Each of us has a deep need for roots, for a sense that we have a place. Part of what's involved in the life of faith is realizing that in the present that need cannot be wholly satisfied. We need to move on, to be ready to go out. We need to learn how to be exiles. Usually this means getting rid of all sorts of clutter—mental and emotional and spiritual baggage to which we're fiercely attached, but which drags us down. "Therefore, since we are surrounded by so great a cloud of witnesses, let us also lay aside every weight, and sin which clings so closely, and let us run with endurance the race that is set before us, looking to Jesus, the founder and perfecter of our faith, who for the joy that was set before him endured the cross, despising the shame, and is seated at the right hand of the throne of God" (12:1–2). Lenten discipline is partly a matter of reminding ourselves of our condition as exiles, making sure that we don't put down our roots too deep, keeping our bags packed and being ready to move on.

Second, we learn how to sojourn in the land of promise by fixing our sights on the horizon: by looking often and hard at the city which God has for us, at the "better country, that is, a heavenly one" (11:16). Christians do this in apparently prosaic ways: praying, coming to church, reading the Bible, pondering and acting out the way of Christ. Yet in doing those things, we become the heirs of Abraham and all those other folk who lived by promises, and so walked before our God. "Therefore God is not ashamed to be called their God, for he has prepared for them a city" (11:16).

And so we pray:

O God, who, calling Abraham to go forth into a country which thou wouldest show him, didst promise that in him all the families of the earth would be blessed; Fulfill thy promise in us, we pray thee, giving us such faith in them as thou shalt count unto us for righteousness, that in us and through us thy purpose may be fulfilled; through Jesus Christ our Lord. Amen.

CHAPTER 19

THE WAY OF HOLINESS

Isaiah 35

The wilderness and the dry land
shall be glad;
the desert shall rejoice
and blossom like the crocus;
it shall blossom abundantly
and rejoice with joy and singing.
The glory of Lebanon
shall be given to it,
the majesty of Carmel
and Sharon.
They shall see the glory of
the LORD,
the majesty of our God.

Strengthen the weak hands,
and make firm the feeble knees.
Say to those who have
an anxious heart,
"Be strong; fear not!
Behold, your God
will come with vengeance,
with the recompense of God.
He will come and save you."

Then the eyes of the blind
shall be opened,
and the ears of the deaf
unstopped;
then shall the lame man
leap like a deer,
and the tongue of the mute
sing for joy.
For waters break forth
in the wilderness,
and streams in the desert;
the burning sand shall become
a pool,
and the thirsty ground
springs of water;
in the haunt of jackals,
where they lie down,
the grass shall become
reeds and rushes.

And a highway shall be there,
and it shall be called
the Way of Holiness;
the unclean shall not pass over it.
It shall belong to those
who walk on the way;
even if they are fools,
they shall not go astray.

No lion shall be there,
nor shall any ravenous beast
come up on it;
they shall not be found there,
but the redeemed
shall walk there.
And the ransomed of the LORD
shall return
and come to Zion with singing;
everlasting joy shall be
upon their heads;
they shall obtain
gladness and joy,
and sorrow and sighing
shall flee away.

Isaiah 35

We often fall into one of two mistakes when we talk about the saints of God. Sometimes we think of saints as a super-breed of believers, a race of genetically modified Christians who grow to gigantic proportions and undertake feats of spiritual heroism that we mortals couldn't possibly aspire to. Or, if we don't have a taste for the legends of the saints, we may instead think of them as possessed of an awesome moral purity which sets them apart from the rest of the human race—unapproachably and almost embarrassingly upright figures whom we may admire but cannot hope to emulate. Both ways of thinking about the saints are common enough, but they don't really serve us very well. What's the problem with these ways of thinking about the saints?

Part of the problem is that they hold saintliness at a distance; saints are utterly unlike anything we might recognize as human in the ways that we are human. And, in a way, that's rather consoling. It lets us off the hook to some extent. Thinking of the saints in these very unrealistic ways actually makes it a great deal easier for us to excuse ourselves from taking the command to saintliness seriously as something addressed to us. We know we aren't superheroes, we know we're only moderately good, and so we can safely pass the responsibility for living a saintly life on to someone else, some larger-than-life figure made for that sort of thing.

But there's a deeper problem. It's that talking of saints as superheroes starts from the wrong place. It starts from our end of things; it suggests that what being a saint is really about is being a bigger, more spectacular, more upright, human being. But it isn't. Sainthood is about God. And the rule in talking about saints, as with talking about most things to do with the Christian gospel, is this: To talk of saints, we need to talk of God.

When we celebrate the saints, we're talking about the human side of something which God does. We're trying to indicate the shape which human life takes on when God speaks and acts and saves. Like the Church, like sacraments, like Scripture, so also with saints: To figure out what's going on, we need to see that the important thing in the end is not the human reality, but God himself, present and active to transfigure and transform. To talk Christianly about saints, then, we need to talk of this God. What do we need to say about him?

The first and most important thing to be said is that God is holy. Saints, holy ones, are what they are because first of all God is himself the holy one. What is this holiness of God? If you want a bit of a definition, I suppose it would be something like this: God's own holiness is the sheer uniqueness of his being. "Who is like you, O Lord, among the gods? Who is like you, majestic in holiness, awesome in glorious deeds, doing wonders?" (Exodus 15:11). It's uniqueness which has to be the leading idea here. When we talk of God's holiness, we aren't talking of him as if he were a straight-laced, buttoned up character, cold and aloof, surveying all our moral muddle and failure with utter distaste. Most of us have met such characters in the ranks of the clergy or schoolmasters, but God isn't one of them, eyeing us all with suppressed moral outrage. No, first of all, God's holiness means God's utter uniqueness, the majestic, undefeated freedom in which he is who he is (Isaiah 40:25). The holy God is particular, segregated, uniquely himself. It's not so much that the holy God has to keep himself from contact with other realities to avoid contamination; it's more that God is absolutely and powerfully distinctive, incomparable. And so when Scripture celebrates God's holiness, it's not simply in order to draw attention to his moral purity, or to explain his hatred of our sins, but in order to say: God is who God is.

Now, it's crucial that we grasp that God's holiness is not solely his own possession. This holy God makes other things holy; he, the holy one, is a God who sanctifies. Above all, God sanctifies his human creation. He sets apart, dedicates people for his own purpose. How does God make people holy? He does so by electing; God the holy one chooses another reality and in so doing separates it out, takes it to himself, and commits himself to fulfill his will for it. God chooses that alongside himself there should be his people, the people who will live with and love and serve and obey and above all praise him. And as God separates, God judges: God the holy one resists and opposes and defeats our resistance and opposition to him, overthrowing it, setting it aside. "For you have died, and your life is hidden with Christ in God" (Colossians 3:3). God overcomes all the obstacles to his great work of sanctifying a people for himself. Further, as God separates, God purifies: God the holy one makes what he chooses into something fitting. He perfects it, making it into what God wills it to be. In all this—in electing, in judging, in purifying—God the holy one creates a human reality which echoes his own holiness, which corresponds in its human way to the sheer perfection of his own being. At the end of this process are the saints of God.

All this may be heavy-duty theology, but it's needful as a way of making sure we hang on to a pretty crucial point which we might otherwise overlook: Saints are what they are because of God. We haven't even begun to understand saintliness unless we see that behind the saints lie the infinite recesses of the life of God himself. If that makes saints a bit less cheerily domestic, it also makes sure we realize that a saint is something very different from an especially successful religious person. Saints aren't those who have got a flair for the life of religion, those who have somehow made an especially fine showing and get top marks in

Christian discipleship. Saintliness simply cannot be cultivated. It's what God does, because of who God is.

It's that thought—that saintliness is what God does, because of who God is—that we need to get our minds and our wills around. If we do that, it'll quietly explode a good deal of what we might otherwise be tempted to say about saints—above all, perhaps, our habit of making saints into magnified human beings, particularly virtuous and high-flying Christians. A number of things might be said to try and settle this idea in our minds.

First, saints are not a special group within the Church—an elite corps, better trained, higher ranking, the real storm-troopers of the gospel. And the reason this isn't true is, simply, that what makes a saint is baptism. Why baptism? Because baptism is that act of God in which God does, indeed, separate, set apart, mark out. Baptism is the point at which the holy God generates the human echo of his own holiness. Baptism is the beginning of the distinctive human way of life which corresponds to God's own distinctiveness. If you're baptized, you're marked out by God as a saint. Whatever else may happen in the Christian life, whatever other acts of virtue or spiritual labor we may perform, in the end they're nothing other than an extension of baptism, that great act of power in which God makes saints. And because baptism is common to all, as one Church of one Lord, then all God's people are saints, sanctified by water and the Spirit.

Second, therefore, being a saint doesn't mean leaving behind or moving beyond the basic practices of the Christian life: repentance and faith. Saints are saints because of God. They are holy because God sanctifies them. So sainthood isn't first and foremost about performance. It's not primarily a matter of achievement. The heart of saintliness is quite the opposite of busy, confident activity; in fact, it's the utter humility of faith which is basic. Faith is primary, because it's in faith that human life corresponds to the grace of God. Faith is that human emptiness which lets God and God's work be, which receives what God is and what God does, which says Yes to God's work of electing and judging and purifying. And faith is never far from repentance, because repentance is just our acknowledgement that, left to ourselves, we work against God's grace, refuse God's mercy, resist God's call. It's not heroics that matter; it's the much harder, much less-attractive business of letting God's judgment, God's claim, have priority in the way in which I order my life.

Third, therefore, saintliness is best thought of, not as a sort of human performance, but as a way of bearing testimony about something which is not me, a way of bearing witness to the holiness of God declared in the gospel and set before us in the coming of Christ and the sending of the Holy Spirit. Sainthood is a matter of transparency. The saint indicates God: "But by the grace of God I am what I am, and his grace toward me was not in vain. On the contrary, I worked harder than any of them, though it was not I, but the grace of God that is with me" (1 Corinthians 15:10).

This is the simplest thing, and yet it is of all things the most difficult. It's difficult because for most of us, most of the time, our lives are afflicted by a fretful self-interest—part pride, part anxiety, part mistrust—that condemns us always to be worrying about keeping ourselves intact. And so we spend so much of our lives patrolling the borders, making sure no one breaks in on us, no one takes us unaware, no one robs us of ourselves. Above all, we take care lest we are interrupted by God. But sainthood is something quite different. It's not born of that restless distrust and anxiety about losing myself. It's born of a realization, brought home to me in baptism, that life is given, not possessed, and that I am therefore free to be transparent to God. I don't lose everything by that—or perhaps we should say that what I do lose is not worth hanging onto. This openness to God, this untroubled readiness to lose myself, is perhaps the greatest mark of all those who walk on the holy way.

Sainthood, because it is about God, is a matter of baptism; of the humility of faith; of bearing testimony to what keeps me in being. Crucially, *all* are called to this. That call is absolute, unconditional, inescapable. And it is so because we have, indeed, been baptized and marked with the sign of Christ. The call is nothing other than the command that we should be what God has appointed us to be, the saints of God.

All of this means that sainthood is quite a bit different from what we might ordinarily think. Look at the figures on the reredos behind the high altar. To me, at least, they look terribly implausible as saints, just because they look so calm and composed, so integrated, so untroubled by God. But saints are troubled—shaken to the core by the miracle of the gospel, disturbed by God's inescapable call. But above all, this means that the saints of God—that is, amazingly, us—stand under a promise. The promise, in Isaiah's words, is this: "Be strong; fear not! Behold, your God will come with vengeance, with the recompense of God. He will come and save you" (35:4). The God who sets people apart and makes them into saints, the God who so intrusively presses the gospel upon us, is the God who comes and saves. This word, Isaiah says, is addressed "to those who have an anxious heart"—to those who can't make sense of what's happening to them, who fear that God has forgotten them, or that God's promises don't seem to turn out. Be strong; fear not.

The saints of God are those who are called to be strong and without fear. This isn't because they're powerful; they aren't. Nor is it because they're strangers to fear; they know it all too well. But they also know that greater than their weakness, greater than their fear, is the fact that God will come and save. So what we celebrate above all when we think of the saints is, quite simply, the *God* of the saints, whose promise to them, and to us, is this: "the ransomed of the Lord shall return and come to Zion with singing; everlasting joy shall be upon their heads; they shall obtain gladness and joy, and sorrow and sighing shall flee away" (35:10). Amen.

CHAPTER 20

YES IN CHRIST

2 Corinthians 1:15–22

Because I was sure of this, I wanted to come to you first, so that you might have a second experience of grace. I wanted to visit you on my way to Macedonia, and to come back to you from Macedonia and have you send me on my way to Judea. Was I vacillating when I wanted to do this? Do I make my plans according to the flesh, ready to say "Yes, yes" and "No, no" at the same time? As surely as God is faithful, our word to you has not been Yes and No. For the Son of God, Jesus Christ, whom we proclaimed among you, Silvanus and Timothy and I, was not Yes and No, but in him it is always Yes. For all the promises of God find their Yes in him. That is why it is through him that we utter our Amen to God for his glory. And it is God who establishes us with you in Christ, and has anointed us, and who has also put his seal on us and given us his Spirit in our hearts as a guarantee.

2 Corinthians 1:15–22

OUR READING FROM THE BEGINNING of 2 Corinthians finds Paul yet again in trouble with his converts. Paul appeared to have quite a talent for getting into fights with the communities which grew from his proclamation of the gospel. His letters to Corinth, especially this second letter, reveal a great deal about this side of Paul's ministry. They also let us see something of his rather conflicted personality. He seemed to contain a rather curious mix of resentment and generosity; he had a deep sense of the authority which God had bestowed on him, as well as a lack of ease in exercising that authority. Above all, he believed that—weak and fragmented as he was—his life and ministry were caught up in the great drama of God's victory over sin. He read his life as a participation in the afflictions of the Messiah, swept up into the woes of the world as it is wrested from the hands of evil and restored to its maker in Jesus Christ. Paul sometimes appeared to be trapped between two things: a sense that his life was at the cutting edge of God's final purposes for the world, and an equal sense of his sheer inadequacy. Of all instruments the least fit, he nevertheless knew himself to be inescapably called to be the bearer of the gospel.

Some of this, I think, finds expression in the opening chapter of 2 Corinthians. Those to whom he was writing seem to have been grumbling that Paul was fickle in making his plans; having promised a visit, he appeared to have changed his mind once if not twice, leaving them not sure where they were. They might well grumble; after all, a visit from the Apostle Paul was a bit more demanding than a polite social call, and would probably involve all manner of moral and spiritual upheaval. Paul's response—a bit defensive, more than a bit irritable—is to insist that he is no inconstant worldling, changing his appointments to suit his present fancy. Quite the opposite: His apostolic behavior manifests the constant, faithful, unchanging character of the gospel which he serves. "Do I make my plans according to the flesh," he asks, "ready to say 'Yes, yes' and 'No, no' at the same time? As surely as God is faithful, our word to you has not been Yes and No" (1:17–18).

It sounds, of course, as if the great apostle is rattled at being called to account for his behavior. And yet as nearly always in Paul, what seems like not much more than a fit of pique turns into an extraordinarily profound statement about the gospel of Jesus Christ. Paul reads his circumstances—even the circumstances of a potential scrap with his converts—in the light of the very basic character of the gospel, and in so doing sets before us a permanent principle of gospel life. The principle is this: "the Son of God, Jesus Christ ... was not Yes and No, but in him it is always Yes. For all the promises of God find their Yes in him" (1:19–20). What's in play here?

First, Paul is unequivocal in insisting that the gospel is the declaration of the constancy or faithfulness of God. His insistence on the point is perhaps not something with which we feel very easy. We have often become used to thinking of the Christian gospel as a sort of hypothesis—as not much more than a good guess about spiritual reality, something which may turn out to be true but also turn out otherwise. But, Paul tells his readers, the gospel is not some kind of fickle Yes or No in that sense—not something arbitrary, something shifting, something lacking in sharpness of outline. It's not just some shapeless hunch. On the contrary, the gospel sets before us something utterly sure, utterly real, absolutely definite. For the gospel declares to us the final fulfillment of the ways and works of God. In the gospel we find ourselves summoned by something irrevocable. We're not in the realm of human decisions, human possibilities. The gospel isn't about men and women trying to figure out God in the only way they know. In the gospel, as Paul sees it, we hear a word which makes a final decision about us. And this is true, says Paul, because the gospel is a transcribing of the constancy of God. Here we have the final display of God's steadiness. The faithfulness which Paul claims about himself as an apostle is therefore nothing other than a reflection of something very basic about the gospel and the God of the gospel: God is true to himself; all his ways are sure; he is not uncertain, or inconstant, or wavering, but the one who in the gospel announces his final word: "Yes."

Second, the sum and substance of the gospel is Jesus Christ. In and as this one, God's final Yes is pronounced; in and as Jesus Christ, God finally demonstrates his truth and constancy. "In him," Paul says, "it is always Yes. For all the promises of God find their Yes in him" (1:19–20). We can't get very far with the message of the Apostle Paul unless we see how deeply his mind and soul are branded with the name of Jesus Christ. Here, in that name and in the one who bears that name, is the animating center of Paul's life as an apostle and the core of the gospel. For Paul, Jesus Christ is not some incidental figure, a character in a larger drama in which other actors also have their parts to play alongside him. On the contrary, he embodies the whole history of God's saving purposes. In him the whole drama has its beginning; he is its theme; in him alone it finds its resolution. Apart from him, there is no history of God with us, no salvation, no savior, no human flourishing.

The great reformer Calvin says in his commentary on 2 Corinthians that Jesus Christ is "the head, the sum, the consummation of all spiritual doctrine," and that takes us to the heart of Paul's point here. Why is there this fierce concentration on Jesus Christ? Because for Paul, the man Jesus is the Son of God. By talking of Jesus in that way, he means something like this: Jesus bears God's being to us; he acts out God's purposes;

he fulfills God's promises, so that in him, God's final Yes is announced to the world.

But what is this Yes, this fulfillment of all God's promises in Jesus Christ? Paul gives expression to a basic Christian conviction that we live in an era of fulfillment rather than an era of expectation. We are, quite simply, not in the dark. We are not those who have some initial sense of who God is and what God wills for us, but still lack a final, clear manifestation of the will and purpose of God. We live in the light. We're those who have seen, those to whom God's final manifestation has come. To think of the Christian gospel as if it were simply one more in a series of manifestations of God, one more attempt to figure out the hidden reality of the world of the divine, is to miss the point pretty radically. One of the basic convictions which animated early Christian faith was a deep sense that in Jesus Christ God had made human life and history "new." And that newness is above all to do with the fact that in Jesus Christ we encounter fulfillment. What was once hidden is now laid bare; what was once anticipated by hints and guesses is now manifest, set before us as one endless divine affirmation.

It's perhaps worth saying that none of this is a matter of Christian arrogance; it's not at all a matter of claiming that we Christians have God pinned down, defined and controllable and all ready for inspection. Nor is it a weapon to be used against those who don't share our point of view. Quite the opposite: The kind of certainty which Paul is talking about here is born not of pride but of amazement. And that amazement—at the staggering fact that God's ways and works do find their fulfillment in the rabbi from Nazareth—finds expression in Paul here in 2 Corinthians: the amazement that in Jesus Christ, and him alone, it is "always Yes" to the promises of God.

Paul is not explicit about which particular promises he has in mind here. What he is really concerned with is the overall shape of God's dealings with humankind. The whole history of God's relation with the human race finds its climactic moment in Jesus. In his life and death and resurrection, in his movement from glory to humiliation and again to lordship at the Father's right hand, the threads of human history are all drawn together and made into one strand. Jesus Christ is therefore the goal of all God's ways with the people of the world—first of all with Israel, to whom the promises of God come in a special way, but through Israel to the whole of humanity. Jesus Christ sums up and perfects God's dealings with God's creation. In him is fulfillment—fulfillment of the promise that God is our God and Father; fulfillment of the promise that our wickedness will not be allowed to destroy the purposes of God; fulfillment of the promise that he is with us in covenant fellowship

So Saint Paul, at the beginning of this second, painful letter to the Christians at Corinth, is stung into reaction by the charge of inconstancy. Here we see Paul's passion—for the gospel, for Jesus Christ as its very essence, for the astounding reality of God's promises fulfilled which the gospel declares. God says Yes, always Yes. There is no wavering, no instability, no hesitancy. We live in the age of the lavish outworking of God's eternal will to be God for us. What difference does this make? For Paul, it makes all the difference in the world. Henceforth, because in Christ all God's promises are fulfilled, human life is one long Amen to God's Yes. "That is why it is through him that we utter our Amen to God for his glory" (1:20). To say Amen is to acknowledge and affirm something which we have heard and which binds us. Saying Amen—at the end of a prayer, at the end of a statement of the gospel—is expressing solemn agreement with something which commits us, which encounters us with the force and authority of God. And Paul is here telling us that the nerve center of being a Christian believer, the heart of discipleship to Jesus Christ, is saying Amen to the fact that in Christ all God's purposes are fulfilled. In him we find the gathering up and perfecting of the ways and works of God, God's great Yes. And to that, we say our own Yes. Here we acquiesce to, ratify, and affirm the great affirmation of the gospel.

How do we make that affirmation? We make it, Paul tells us, "through him, through Christ." We don't do it with energy of our own. We make this affirmation because through Christ we are enabled to do it. Our Yes to God's Yes, our glad acknowledgment that God's promises are fulfilled in him, is something which Jesus Christ works in us, completing the circle of his own fulfillment of the promises of God. *Where* do we make this affirmation? Primarily, in worship. When we gather for the praise of God, hearing his Word and receiving the tokens of his mercy in the sacraments, we simply say Yes! Over and above all our talking and singing and praying, all our struggles to get worship right and make it deep and meaningful, there is the most primary thing which worship does: affirm God's Yes, let it stand for itself, praise it, reiterate it. But we also say Yes to God in obedience, as we take upon ourselves the pattern of life which reflects God's truth. To live a life of Christian obedience is not primarily to struggle to be better, or to match up to some image of ourselves as morally clean. To live the Christian life is simply to say Yes, to let God be all in all, to concur with God's great declaration in the gospel that his promises find their culmination in Jesus.

In word and deed, in speech and action, then, we utter our Amen to God. If there is a conclusion to draw here, it is this. Christian wisdom consists in letting God be God, in hearing and consenting to God's great declaration in the gospel that the time is fulfilled, the end of the ages has come, and salvation, fulfillment, peace are established in our midst. Christian wisdom consists in lining ourselves up with that truth. In one sense there aren't any great depths to the Christian life—no mystical doctrines to learn, no tricks of the spiritual life to master, no experiences to cultivate. What there is instead is the quiet, daily business of setting our hearts on what God has done for us. We are to love what God is and what God has done; we are to direct our lives toward him as our goal, and to make him our supreme delight and joy. And we are to learn that in our praises and our daily living, our chief task is this: to echo in what we say and what we do that great Yes which God speaks in his Son, and to find in him none other than the way of life. To do that is to utter the Amen through him, and to begin to live to the glory of God.

Part V

PRESSING ON

CHAPTER 21

THE HEART OF PERSEVERANCE

Revelation 2:1–7

To the angel of the church in Ephesus write: "The words of him who holds the seven stars in his right hand, who walks among the seven golden lampstands.

"I know your works, your toil and your patient endurance, and how you cannot bear with those who are evil, but have tested those who call themselves apostles and are not, and found them to be false. I know you are enduring patiently and bearing up for my name's sake, and you have not grown weary. But I have this against you, that you have abandoned the love you had at first. Remember therefore from where you have fallen; repent, and do the works you did at first. If not, I will come to you and remove your lampstand from its place, unless you repent. Yet this you have: you hate the works of the Nicolaitans, which I also hate. He who has an ear, let him hear what the Spirit says to the churches. To the one who conquers I will grant to eat of the tree of life, which is in the paradise of God."

Revelation 2:1–7

THE LETTERS TO THE SEVEN churches in the early chapters of the Apocalypse are best read as what they claim to be: as what the Spirit says to the churches. In each of the letters, John the seer is instructed by the risen Christ to write a letter to what's called the angel of seven different churches—which is probably a way of saying that he is to address the words to the presiding spirit of each community. The words he writes are a dissection of the church to which they are addressed, a judgment in which the truth about the community and its fidelity to Christ is examined and declared. If we are to grasp what is going on in these strange passages, we have to understand that the words of the seer are not his own; they are given, and given by the Lord Christ himself. His messages are apostolic messages: They are the speech of Christ himself, through the instrument of John. In them, we are to hear the Spirit—that is, in them we are to hear the risen and glorified Christ who is not absent and mute but present and communicative, addressing his Church in the Spirit's power. There is a twofold assumption behind these passages: that Jesus Christ is with us, and that he is a speaker. In the strange symbolic language of our passage, Jesus Christ "walks among the seven golden lampstands" (Revelation 2:1)—that is, he is present and active, striding among the communities of the Church as their Lord and Sustainer and Judge. And as such, his voice sounds forth, speaking the words of the one from whose mouth (we have learned at the beginning of Revelation) there issues a sharp two-edged sword, which is the Word of God.

In all their unfamiliarity, these letters are an immense resource for us, for a couple of reasons. First, they are full of a vivid sense that taking the Christian faith seriously means membership in a community, and in a particular kind of community—a fellowship in which Jesus Christ is surely alive and present, among which he moves with freedom and authority and grace; a fellowship which is not just a human assembly but a gathering around this radiant and eloquent and mobile presence of Christ. "Behold," this one says, "I am alive forevermore" (1:18). That in itself ought to be enough to jolt us out of our familiar ways of thinking about the Church, by making us see it is not just an enclave of the religiously like-minded, but the congregation brought together by the fact that he, Jesus Christ, is and speaks.

Second, these letters are also filled with an acute awareness of the distinction between the Church and the world. It's basic to the way in which these letters think about the Church that there is a distinctiveness about the community which attends to Jesus Christ. That distinctiveness is always under threat from inside and outside the Church, and the peace and well-being of the Church depend in part on not letting that distinctiveness get traded away. To read what is said here, then, will instruct us, too, as we try to negotiate our own cultural circumstances and discern the points at which faithfulness to Christ will press us to say "no" to our culture.

For the Apocalypse as a whole, and the letters to the seven churches in particular, the life of the Church and of individual disciples of Christ is always a field of conflict. The conflict is variously portrayed—between Babylon and Jerusalem, between Satan and the elect, but always between God and sin. Christian fellowship and discipleship are episodes in the conflict between God and evil. Because the Christian life is thought of in these conflictual terms—as a struggle with forces which seek to undermine and break down life in fellowship with Christ—then one of the key virtues in the letters is that of perseverance or endurance.

"I know," Christ says to the church at Ephesus, "you are enduring patiently and bearing up for my name's sake, and you have not grown weary" (2:3). The endurance which Revelation has in mind is this: It is a holding fast to the confession that Christ really is present, really does direct the ways of humankind, really does speak and rule. To endure in this way involves a setting of mind, heart and will in a constant direction. It involves a focusing of our lives and a certain exclusiveness—a refusal to heed other voices, a resistance against losing direction by spending too much time looking at the view.

Above all, endurance is bound up with undivided allegiance to Christ. The Christian who perseveres is one who is clear that no new set of circumstances, no change in the frame of the world, however enticing or authoritative, can ever cause us to change track. The persevering Christian knows one reality above all: the reality of Christ, his name, his presence, his governance, his dealings with us. Faithfully to do the business which we are called to do, to fulfill our calling as his disciples, is simply, as Revelation puts it, to bear up for his name's sake (2:3)—to live and act constantly by the truth and goodness of his name, to keep going because he is.

Such endurance is threatened, both from outside and from within. It's threatened from outside because the world finds the Christian's perseverance troublesome. It's not only that the world finds it ludicrous, a sort of ignorant and compulsive pigheadedness. It's also that the world, when it's got its wits about it, realizes that the Christian's perseverance shows up the world's own disorder and unrighteousness and instability. Even though these Christians may look a foolish lot, doggedly hanging on to their gospel, their very fidelity is a challenge to the world's ways. And because that's so, the witness of Christian perseverance must be broken in some way. It has to be muted, or softened, or absorbed, or even if necessary silenced, so that the world can be left to fritter away its life undisturbed. And how does the world do that? By charming, or bribing, or cajoling or bullying the Christian community, by seducing or harassing it in some way or other so that the intensity and persistence with which it holds fast to the name of Christ will be breached. Endurance generates affliction as part of the tribulation which the Church of Christ will have in the world.

But endurance is also threatened from within. Endurance involves long-term resistance. It means that those who hold fast to the name of Christ have made a decision in advance that they will not enjoy certain kinds of fulfillment, and will exclude from their lives the circumstances which would offer those kinds of fulfillment. And a commitment like that, made in ignorance of what will happen to us in the future, binding us for all our lives, makes us weary. We look around at our neighbors who have not made the same commitment, and they seem so much richer and freer and more supple than we are, so much more yielding and able to be themselves in such interesting and absorbing ways. And we begin to wonder if we might be able to ease up a bit—if we might, perhaps, be able to give ourselves a bit of space. Maybe we don't need to be so insistent on the name of Christ? Might it not be that there is a place for other names alongside his, making a little claim on our lives and releasing us of this burden of being so separate and odd? And so, because we've been making our confession so long and are a bit tired of it all, we ease up, and allow things to slide.

These threats, external and internal, to the perseverance of Christian communities and their members are very real and very perilous. That's why here in Revelation they evoke such a terrible judgment: "You have abandoned the love you had at first" (2:4). Not to endure is to abandon our first love for Christ, his name and his gospel. How should that love be characterized? It involves, most of all, a cleaving to Christ as the one whose name alone is salvation, life, and peace. Put at its simplest, Christian faith is love of that reality, love of the name of Christ and what it signifies.

Such love, if it is deep and genuine, necessarily involves the Christian in separation from the world, because love is exclusive, and divided love is no love at all. And separation, once again, evokes the world's censure and opposition. "If you were of the world," Christ tells his disciples in the Gospel of John, "the world would love you as its own; but because you are not of the world, but I chose you out of the world, therefore the world hates you" (15:19). It's precisely this hatred, this open or hidden animosity, which is the world's weapon against Christian perseverance. Whether from fear or from lack of confidence or from excessive love of comfort and approval, we try to soften the world's odium by dividing our love. To do so, we half-realize, is wicked infidelity, an abandonment of our first love of God. Yet we continue: Remarkably quickly, we give up our commitments, telling ourselves that all we're doing is growing up a bit, maturing beyond those absurd polarities with which we began, mellowing into generosity. In fact, however, we are renouncing our love and the tasks that it sets before us, and separating ourselves from the life of Christ.

"I have this against you, that you have abandoned the love you had at first" (2:4). What is to be done in this situation? Here are the seer's words from the risen Christ: "Remember therefore from where you have fallen; repent, and do the works you did at first" (2:5). If the threat to Christian endurance is to be countered, it has to be by being jolted into awareness of just what is happening. We need somehow to come to a true reckoning about ourselves, to see ourselves for what we are. That means that the consolations and evasions and excuses with which we have clothed our drift away from God need to be broken apart. We need to see that we have fallen; and to see that, we need to set our present against our past—to measure our present inconstancy by our past resolution. This, we must see, is what we have become; this is what we have made of ourselves. If we do that, then we are on the road to repentance, able to turn away from the realm of unrighteousness and vacillation and compromise, and back toward the name of Christ. But repentance is a matter not only of intention but of action; it involves a renewal of active obedience, a consent to the will of God which is practical. "Do the works you did at first" (2:5).

Remembrance, repentance, the renewal of the works of faith—all this is involved in recovery of the love of Christ in which we must patiently endure. Yet in and of themselves, they are not enough. Indeed, if we start with them we just condemn ourselves to failure, for the problem is precisely that we cannot and will not remember, repent and renew our lives. In the matter of endurance, therefore, we cannot place ourselves in our hands; we are powerless against the threats to which we are exposed. But—crucially—Christ is not powerless. In those curious words at the beginning of our lesson, Christ "holds the seven stars in his right hand," and "walks among the seven golden lampstands" (2:1). Christ himself holds his Church in his hand. The lives of these apparently fragile communities are grasped by Christ in the right hand of his sovereign rule over all things; he is their Lord, and therefore their protector. And not only that, but he is present to them. He walks among the lampstands—that is, he is present.

And what does all this say about the matter of Christian endurance or perseverance? It says this: In all the threats that attend the Christian life—threats of opposition, threats of compromise, threats of simply giving up from exhaustion—we are to turn not to ourselves, but to the Lord Christ, who is with us as king and savior. He alone, the Church's Lord, is our help. Only he can protect us against the world, and only he can protect us against ourselves. Without him we cannot hope to endure; without him we cannot bear up, and will simply grow weary and lose our way. But we are not without him. He is our strength and our shield.

In practical terms, this means that at the heart of perseverance in the life of faith is invocation of God. If we would endure, we must learn to ask God to help us in our weakness. Listen to Psalm 142:

With my voice I cry out to the Lord;
with my voice I plead for mercy to the Lord.
I pour out my complaint before him;
I tell my trouble before him.
When my spirit faints within me,
you know my way!
In the path where I walk
they have hidden a trap for me.
Look to the right and see:
there is none who takes notice of me;
no refuge remains to me;
no one cares for my soul.
I cry to you, O Lord;
I say, "You are my refuge,
my portion in the land of the living."
Attend to my cry,
for I am brought very low!
Deliver me from my persecutors,
for they are too strong for me!
Bring me out of prison,
that I may give thanks to your name!
The righteous will surround me,
for you will deal bountifully with me.

Apart from that prayer there is no hope for the Church's endurance or for the endurance of any one of its members. But the Lord Christ is among us, and he hears our prayers, and will answer them. Let us therefore look to him in whom alone we may endure. And let us render praise to him who with the Father and the Son is worshiped and glorified, now and forever. Amen.

CHAPTER 22

ENDURANCE

Matthew 10:16–23

Behold, I am sending you out as sheep in the midst of wolves, so be wise as serpents and innocent as doves. Beware of men, for they will deliver you over to courts and flog you in their synagogues, and you will be dragged before governors and kings for my sake, to bear witness before them and the Gentiles. When they deliver you over, do not be anxious how you are to speak or what you are to say, for what you are to say will be given to you in that hour. For it is not you who speak, but the Spirit of your Father speaking through you. Brother will deliver brother over to death, and the father his child, and children will rise against parents and have them put to death, and you will be hated by all for my name's sake. But the one who endures to the end will be saved. When they persecute you in one town, flee to the next, for truly, I say to you, you will not have gone through all the towns of Israel before the Son of Man comes.

Matthew 10:16–23

Any modern Christian reading the 10th chapter of Matthew is bound to feel a certain unease. Listening to the story of Jesus sending out the apostles and hearing his clear words on the inevitability of rejection, we are brought up short against the fact that this is not a world where we feel at home. Its picture of the Christian in affliction, and of the necessary and normal character of this affliction, is very strange for us in the Christian West. I doubt that many of us feel like sheep in the midst of wolves or that our life has been marred by the hatred of others. In the settled forms which our Christian lives take, Matthew's picture of Jesus is very foreign indeed.

Christians in other times and places, of course, see things differently. Throughout the history of the Church there have been those for whom opposition, persecution and martyrdom have been a given part of the life of the Church and of discipleship, and running away from those realities has been considered a failure to grasp what it is that the gospel requires of us. Indeed, to give in under persecution and pay one's dues to paganism was simply to put oneself outside the realm of salvation. That in itself ought to make us pause and ask whether all is, in fact, well with us: Is our distance from the world of Matthew 10 just a matter of the passage of time, of shifting into an established Christian culture? Or is it an indication of decline, a pointer to our failure to catch on to something essential to the Christian condition? At the very least, it's worth reflecting that our settled forms of Christianity do not always serve us well. If civil religion undermines our authenticity, it is because established forms of Christian life often succumb to the temptation to soften the contrast between the children of light and the children of darkness; they rather too quickly make the Church's conflict with the world into not much more than an occasional scrap.

Above all, they make it terribly hard for us to see that being a Christian means participating in the shame of Jesus before his persecutors.

If all this is so, then reading what Matthew has to say here will inevitably mean going against the grain of our expectations. This in itself is no bad thing. Luther once spoke of the Bible as our adversary, and that's something we are to bear in mind whenever we turn to Scripture. In an important way, it is hostile to us. It is unfriendly to our use of it as a source book for familiar or consoling truths. It refuses to conform. And in the matter of the affliction of the Christian, this is particularly the case because Scripture—in the psalms, the Gospels, and the Epistles—does not allow us to have the consolations of God without the affliction in the midst of which those consolations are to be found. This doesn't, of course, mean that we are to read Scripture as unrelieved bad news—quite the opposite. But it does mean that part of listening for the good news is being prepared for more than a little disturbance.

Matthew's vision of the Christian community sees affliction as a basic ingredient in the Christian life. Why is this so? Why does Jesus tell us with alarming simplicity and authority that we will be hated by all? He speaks of a particular kind of affliction. He is not speaking here of the kind of affliction which flows from the natural clash of personalities, the kind of opprobrium which one person heaps on another out of sheer inhuman lovelessness or contempt. However much that may form part of the experience of Christian affliction, more is meant here. The "more" is this: The disciples of Jesus will be hated *for his name's sake*, that is, because of who Jesus is.

The affliction of the Christian is a reaction against the Lord of the Christian; the Christian attracts the opposition of the world because the Christian is a bearer of the name of Christ. We stand in his company; we are in his fellowship; our *being with him is the* determining factor of our existence. And so around us there gathers that resistance which also marked him out and finally put him away; the shadow of rejection falls on the disciples, too. Most especially is this the case, Matthew tells us, because not only do the disciples keep company with the rejected Lord, but they are commissioned to speak in his name. The disciples are sent out, charged by the Lord, given authority and commanded not to remain silent, but to speak about the gospel. And speaking the gospel means getting caught up in the unyielding reality of human rejection of God. Just so, Jesus tells us, you will be hated.

Why does the good news of the peaceful and wholesome kingdom of God issue in rejection? Essentially because that kingdom is a direct onslaught on the autonomy of the world. It is a final and undefeatable challenge to the great illusion that the world and we the people of the world are competent to run our own affairs. God's kingdom is God assuming the reins of history. And that means that there must be repentance. Faced with God's kingdom, with his sovereign taking hold of human life, we all stand under an absolute requirement: the requirement of complete and radical reorientation. Repentance means much more than admission of guilt. It means total redirection, becoming a new person—above all, looking to God and his kingdom as the one truth which alone is to be the center of human life and affection. The apostles don't simply proclaim the need for moral reformation; rather, in proclaiming repentance, they proclaim the need for new birth. And there is an urgency to this proclamation. God's kingdom is *at hand* (Matthew 4:17); it is not a distant prospect, a moral imperative or a hope. It is here—insistently, urgently, finally among us.

The urgency is expressed in the command that the apostles should travel unencumbered, attached to nothing and weighed down by nothing. The finality is expressed in the terrible prophetic sign which they are to give to those who refuse to hear: "shake off the dust from your feet" (Matthew 10:14). Declare them, that is, to be those who have set themselves in opposition to the rule of God, who have heard the summons to repentance but have simply stayed where they are and refused to budge. But to indicate the kingdom of God in this way means that the apostles share in the hostility and rejection which is the lot of those who declare the demands of the gospel. Matthew's picture of the reception of the apostles is indeed pretty bleak—the steadfast opposition of political and religious authorities, the breakdown of natural bonds of affection, the letting loose of *hatred*.

The disciple of Jesus Christ just does not fit in. The disciple hasn't made peace with the world, hasn't settled down into a more or less peaceful co-existence; the disciple is always troubled by life as he or she encounters it—not because it isn't good, and certainly not because the disciple doesn't know how to be human, but because the disciple senses, with greater or lesser clarity, that something is *wrong*. What others think is self-evident, the disciple is disposed to doubt; what others cheerfully dismiss as outmoded or regressive or just simple-minded, the disciple might well take very seriously. For the disciple doesn't conform; more than that, the disciple repudiates the way things go on, setting aside one way of life and embracing another very different possibility. And in so doing, the disciple isn't guided by some personal principle of non-compliance, and isn't giving vent to a particularly feisty personality.

The disciple's nonconformity has its roots in the astonishing reality which is at the heart of Jesus' proclamation: "the kingdom of heaven is at hand" (Matthew 4:17; 10:7). The disciple knows what others do not know or choose not to know—that God is invading the world, that the world is governed by the rule of God in Jesus. And the disciple therefore denies the suggestion that we can ignore God's rule without losing ourselves; and so the disciple protests. He or she doesn't remain silent or inactive, but rather speaks and acts in ways which attest to the fact that in Jesus God has struck the decisive blow against evil and made all things new.

And so, Matthew tells us, the disciple individually and the company of disciples together are afflicted. It's important that we realize that affliction is something which characterizes the Church as a whole, not just a few individuals within it. Affliction defines the Church. As soon as it ceases to be harassed, as soon as the pressures ease and the Church feels it can look around itself with a measure of satisfaction, then it's time for vigilance—an especial vigilance that the gospel remains supreme. For the Church is built on the gospel, and confessing the gospel—speaking the name of Jesus—always carries with it the threat of rejection. Testimony and martyrdom are very close, and there was a truth in those strands of early Christianity which made the martyr (not the bishop) the real mark of Christian authenticity in the assembly of the people of God.

What does this mean for the disciple's manner of life? Three things are worth bearing in mind here.

First, "beware of men" (Matthew 10:17). This does not, of course, mean that the Christian is to adopt some kind of principled misanthropy, some sour cynicism or distrust of others. What it does counsel is an honest, truthful awareness of the fact that human life is as the gospel describes it to be: a place where God and sin collide. Christians are not to expect that their faith will find confirmation in the orders of human society; nor may they hope to be congratulated for bringing to perfection all that is beautiful and good and true according to the best lights of the world.

Particularly from our place as an established church, we have real difficulty in keeping our thinking straight here. We have been very quick to baptize (both babies and social conventions); we have been slow to prophesy, and even slower to divest ourselves of the kind clutter of prestige which makes discipleship so hard. More than that, we have often expressed surprise when obedience to the gospel has brought opposition—as if somehow we had forgotten that the joy of the gospel will often be a sword which divides. We need to learn again that the disciple is to prepare for conflict—not to be perturbed by it, but to understand it as the natural state of affairs for those who find their way through life by obedience to Jesus.

This wariness requires a kind of spiritual and human maturity which is not easy to attain. This is because, second, the disciple is required to undertake life with a curious mix of astute wisdom and unprotected harmlessness. "Be wise as serpents and innocent as doves" (Matthew 10:16). The wisdom of the snake (always a tricky creature in the Bible) is to know how to wriggle out of trouble, and the disciple needs a dash of worldly prudence. But prudence is not the same as cunning or sharp dealing, and so the disciple is also to demonstrate the harmlessness, even helplessness, of the dove. He is to repudiate worldly wisdom and strength, to put no reliance on whatever gifts of clever turns of phrase or fancy footwork might be available. No, the disciple is among wolves and, like the sheep, ill-equipped for the situation. There is, indeed, a proper *powerlessness* which is to mark the disciple of Jesus. And this is because at the heart of the gospel's mystery is the passion. It is in the passion—in Jesus' silence, in his refusal to be goaded into lashing out at his tormentors—that the world's healing is won; it is in the fellowship of his sufferings that the disciple keeps company with the Lord.

Beware; suffer; and, third, *endure*. Christian endurance is the steady refusal to let the world's contradiction of the gospel grind one down. It is patiently continuing to keep company with Jesus despite that fact that most others think of one as embarrassingly zealous, earnest or uncompromising, as a vulgar survival of mythology, or as just in the way. Endurance involves a setting of the will, a flinty hardness such as Ezekiel is exhorted to adopt. But it also involves something more than just a tenaciously held decision. It involves a deep sense of the truth and reality and goodness of the realities of the Christian faith, a sense that they are more important than anything in the world. And it also involves a sense that—whatever hole we may find ourselves in—we are accompanied by the living Christ.

Perhaps all this is a bit abstract. For many Christians, even in this century, these things have been lived reality. One such believer was a largely unknown Lutheran pastor, Heinrich Vogel—later to become a great Berlin professor, but at that point tucked away in a small-town parish. In 1937, with the dark closing in on the church in Germany, he wrote a little book on the Apostles Creed, at the beginning of which he wrote this:

> In a world hostile to God, a Christian's life is one of conflict. In life and death he is at war with a most powerful enemy, and would certainly be lost had not his Lord long ago won the battle for him, and daily wins it anew in his stead. In our own day, moreover, there has broken out a totalitarian struggle in which the decision for or against Christ has got to be made. All who bear Christ's name are called to the barricades; all who confess the name of Christ ... are called to a path which is no longer one of safety.

You will be hated by all for my name's sake, Jesus tells us; but he who endures to the end will be saved.

CHAPTER 23

WAITING PATIENTLY

James 5:7–11

Be patient, therefore, brothers, until the coming of the Lord. See how the farmer waits for the precious fruit of the earth, being patient about it, until it receives the early and the late rains. You also, be patient. Establish your hearts, for the coming of the Lord is at hand. Do not grumble against one another, brothers, so that you may not be judged; behold, the Judge is standing at the door. As an example of suffering and patience, brothers, take the prophets who spoke in the name of the Lord. Behold, we consider those blessed who remained steadfast. You have heard of the steadfastness of Job, and you have seen the purpose of the Lord, how the Lord is compassionate and merciful.

James 5:7–11

PATIENCE IS THE VIRTUE in which we allow our lives to run their allotted course in their allotted time. As we exercise patience, we let our lives and the lives of others follow the path which has been laid down for them, without railing against the constraints which that imposes on us. Patience is the virtue of waiting. It involves waiting for all things to reach their end—waiting for others, as well as for ourselves, to take the time they need, and above all waiting for God to fulfill his purposes in his own good time. Patience is the virtue which encounters frustration with a calm and steady frame, waiting steadfastly for time to be fulfilled.

One way of helping us think a bit more deeply about patience is to contrast it with its opposites. Patience is most obviously contrasted with impatience. When we are impatient, we get agitated because we cannot be in complete control of our time. Things don't happen in the way and at the pace that we want them to happen, and so we get aggravated. It can be trivial things: Trains and letters don't arrive when they should; meetings last forever; colleagues exasperate us by talking endlessly and failing to get the point; and we are reduced to fury at the fact that we are subject to these frustrations. More seriously, we can be deeply frustrated with our particular set of circumstances. We may find that our work, or our family, or our social context fills us with profound dismay, and we want to put an end to such frustrations and yet cannot. Or we may be thoroughly dissatisfied with ourselves—disappointed and angry at our limits, whether they are the limits inflicted by others or simply the confines of our character. Impatience is precisely that: our anger directed against the fact that we are hemmed in by ourselves and by others and by our situation, and so find that a measure of fulfillment is denied to us. And so we smolder with only half-concealed annoyance at what inhibits us.

But alongside this, there is another form of the absence of patience: not a refusal to wait, but a sullen, slothful resignation. Faced with the limits we experience, faced with the fact that we cannot be masters of our time and situation, we just give up. We no longer even try to be alert, expectant, attentive; we no longer turn our spirits to the future and allow it to school us in dealing with the present, but we become listless, sluggish, dilatory. Impatience rails against limits; resignation abandons itself to them, and in so doing abandons hope and is overcome by apathy and indifference. "Why bother?" we say; nothing will change, struggling has no effect, so we might just as well slip into a leaden, lifeless passivity.

But both impatience and resignation are sicknesses of the spirit. They are sicknesses because they are untruthful; they fail to see and experience what human life really is in the light of God. Lived in the light of God, our lives can flourish within the inevitable limits of being human. Patience is the particular virtue which acknowledges that those limits of time and situation are not some dreadful enemy which we have to master, but the shape which our lives are given as they follow the path which is laid out for us by God. "Be patient," the letter of James tells us (5:7). The command to patience requires that we wait, and in so doing acknowledge and give assent to the fact that our lives are limited. We are limited by others; we are limited by our own particular characters and endowments; we are limited by the fact that we exist in time, so that certain desires cannot be fulfilled. And patience is the word we have for accepting and living in those limits.

As we exercise patience, we are literally "patient"—that is, we *suffer* or submit to that which we have to undergo because it is part of our condition. We can no more escape it than we can escape from time and space altogether and become gods, however much we would like to do so. But, crucially, this kind of patience is not mere surrender or hopeless compliance. It's rooted in the fact that we know something about ourselves and the world. Very simply, we know Jesus Christ. We know that he was, and is, and is to come. We know that over and above all constraints, frustrations and disappointments, he is. And because we know that, then it also is given to us to know something else. We know that because of Jesus Christ our lives have a very definite shape and move in a very definite direction. What makes it so hard for us to exercise patience is that we fear that there is no shape and direction, and so we must impose that direction ourselves, taking charge of our time to make sure it is not overrun by aggravations. But those who know Jesus Christ and trust in him need have no fear in this matter. Why? Because, as James tells his readers, "you have seen the purpose of the Lord" (5:11). Those who trust in Jesus Christ and live their lives in fellowship with him are given to know that our time is not just one frustration after another; it's the space which is given to us by God, the space in which we may fulfill God's calling. Our lives are not just an indefinite thing, a void, always being invaded by hostile forces, always somewhere we have to patrol to beat away transgressors. Rather, our lives are shapely; they have a direction; they follow a path. And that path leads us, as James puts it, to "the coming of the Lord" (5:7). What does he mean?

We can be patient only if we have a measure of trustful confidence about our lives. Patience requires a certain steadiness of spirit, a steadfastness, in which we keep on keeping on, not out of sheer listlessness or doggedness, but because we think our time has a *telos*, a goal. For the disciples of Jesus Christ, that goal is his coming. To trust in that coming is to trust the fact that our lives will not finally be ruined or cast down. The purpose of God will be fulfilled; Jesus Christ will come and will establish unambiguously and authoritatively what God the Father wills for his creatures. On the way, we will be frustrated; we will experience all sorts of minor irritations and major afflictions; we will often enough fear that the Lord may have no purpose. But in the middle of all that the patient Christian knows that the Lord is coming, and that nothing can deflect that divine purpose. For that purpose which gathers up our lives into itself is rooted in the unshakable will of God; he has determined it, and so it will be.

Patience, then, is rooted in knowing that our lives are purposeful. This knowledge of the end of our lives helps us get a different perspective on our present condition—for we have seen not only "the purpose of the Lord," James says, but also "how the Lord is compassionate and merciful" (5:11). The patient Christian sees the world as a different place from the impatient or slothful person. Impatience and sloth take the world to be a great thicket of irritations and setbacks. Patience helps us see that the world is the place of God's compassion and mercy. God gives us our lives; he allots to us our particular space, our particular time, in all their limitedness. He gives us this particular set of circumstances—these people, this background, this calling, this personality, this collection of abilities and inabilities. And in so doing, God teaches us to think of our lives not just as an obstacle course to battle against, but as a place where we are met by his compassion and mercy. God's compassion and mercy are in these things.

This does not, of course, tell us *how* God's mercy and compassion are to be encountered. It certainly does not mean that we have to accept patiently everything that comes our way just because it comes our way. There is a time for impatience, for protest, for holy unrest; there are limitations which are wicked and against which we must struggle. But we struggle against them precisely because we know Jesus Christ, because we know the purpose of the Lord, and so our protest is not mere resentment but steadfastness, striving for the manifestation of God's end for our lives. Because the world is full of God's compassion and mercy, because our lives are pointed by God to their true end, because we may truthfully wait for these things, then we must also set aside all that obscures that truth, so that patience may flourish.

Patience, then, is waiting on God, knowing that he has secured and will secure our lives. In God we can rest. Patience is an especially important social virtue; indeed, it is one of the most distinguishing features of the fellowship of Christ's people. Whatever else the saints ought to be, they ought to be a patient community. And that means they ought to be patient with each other. The patience of the saints is one of the ways in which the gospel converts us away from our sins and restores us to human fellowship. Impatience eats away at friendship and neighborliness. When we are impatient with our fellows, we refuse to let them be what they are. We want them to think differently, to be capable in the way we think they ought to be capable, to match our ideas about what they should do and how and when they should do it. We are impatient with the elderly because we think they are slow; we are impatient with children because we think they fumble; we are impatient with teenagers because we think they are headstrong and unbiddable. But our impatience is in the end a refusal to let our fellows be, a refusal to allow them the time and space that they need to fulfill God's calling of them. When I'm impatient, I want my neighbor to exist on my terms, in my space, in my time frame. And so, in the end, I lack love—for love is patient. It waits. It looks not to my selfish ideas of what I want from or for my neighbor, but to my neighbor's real end, which is in God. And so, patient love lets my neighbor be. That doesn't mean that we are absolved from any responsibility to our neighbors; quite the contrary—we must act in our neighbor's regard, sometimes intervening, sometimes correcting or challenging. But if we do so, it is not to line up our neighbor with our view of what he or she ought to be, but in order to lovingly and patiently promote the purpose of God.

Such patience goes against the grain. For it means that we have to learn that our fellows are to become what God wills, not what we would like. Unlearning our cherished ideas about what our fellows should be, and unlearning the impatience which so often results from that, is one of the great disciplines of all kinds of human fellowship—churches, academic communities, families, marriages. As we set out to work at that kind of discipline, we soon discover that we are not very good at it—indeed, that we are very bad at it. As James says, we grumble at one another, murmuring and complaining because other people don't do what they should (4:11, 5:9).

It's not just that patience does not come easily to us; it's more that it doesn't come at all, for it is very far outside the range of our abilities. And that is why patience is a fruit of the Holy Spirit. If there is patience in human life and fellowship, it's not because of any capacity that we sinners have; it's because God himself in the power of the Spirit quickens us. The Spirit is God himself making us into what we are not, God himself bestowing upon us the capacity to do what sin prevents us from doing. And that's why, as Micah puts it, we have to "look to the Lord" (7:7). That looking to God, confident that God will hear us, is at the heart of the Christian life, and so is the root of patience.

One last thing: Patience is a path to happiness. "We count them happy which endure," says James (5:11 KJV). The patient, those who endured and waited for the coming of the Lord, were blessed with happiness. Why so? Because patience takes away from us that evil restlessness which is the opposite of waiting for God. Patience means freedom. It means freedom from the burden of frustration and disappointment. It gives us the real, deep freedom of accepting that we are who we are and where we are, and that in those things we discover the purpose of God. It liberates us from the myth that we can flourish only if we are somehow set free from all constraints and all inhibitions—from all those people and situations and hindrances that press in upon us. Patience schools us to find in those limits the necessary form of our lives, and so the way in which we can be truly ourselves. And that is happiness. It's not morose resignation; it's not abandonment of hope; it's happiness in which even now, in the midst of all that comes our way, we know ourselves to be on the path to fulfillment in God. We know the purpose of God; patiently we wait for it; and so by the Spirit's generosity we are given the gift of happiness.

And so we pray:

> *Teach us, O gracious Lord, to begin our works with fear, to go on with obedience, and to finish them in love, and then to wait patiently in hope, and with cheerful confidence to look to thee, whose promises are faithful and rewards infinite; through Jesus Christ our Lord. Amen.*

CHAPTER 24

CHRISTIAN CONTENTMENT

Philippians 4:11b–13

I have learned in whatever situation I am to be content. I know how to be brought low, and I know how to abound. In any and every circumstance, I have learned the secret of facing plenty and hunger, abundance and need. I can do all things through him who strengthens me.

Philippians 4:11b–13

What does Paul mean here by contentment? One way to begin pondering the issue is to say a bit about what he *doesn't* mean. Clearly for Paul contentment is quite different from *comfort*. Contentment isn't the cozy sense of well being that comes from being in a good situation in life. It's not just a matter of being settled, looking at ourselves with the cheerful feeling that we've been spared serious troubles. Contentment isn't just "feeling safe," because contentment as Paul sees it here isn't to be equated with the absence of those things which chafe us and weigh us down. Paul's contentment isn't fair-weather buoyancy. It's contentment in the midst of trouble, contentment while being abased, facing hunger, coping with want. Put simply, content is not *ease*, but a way of facing *unease*, a way of not being crushed by vexation, however grievous and troublesome.

But if that's true, it's also true that contentment in Paul's sense is not a matter of self-sufficiency. Being content is not mastering our fate, rising above circumstances by independence and self-reliance. Paul's contentment is apostolic. The resources for it aren't derived from within; he doesn't attain contentment through the best use of his own powers, refusing to let himself be swallowed up by circumstance and instead acting out of a sufficiency within himself. On the contrary, Paul's contentment derives from God. It's not a matter of human strength of character; it's a matter of human weakness transfigured by the astonishing sufficiency of God. Contentment is that exercise of faith in which we accept the sufficiency of God. It's not feeling all right; it's not mastery of circumstance. It's the fruit of the conversion of our lives to the grace and goodness of God.

All this begins to point us to the really vital nerve of Christian contentment. Its true root, its real energy, is faith. Faith is resting on God, acknowledging and trusting and abandoning myself to the reality of God outside me. Contentment, therefore, is not about me, about what I can do to adjust my mind to the troubles and terrors of being human. True contentment, rooted in faith, is grounded in something which is outside me, grounded in the reality of God, known in faith, trusted in faith. It's not poise or self-mastery, but self-abandonment. Contentment happens when my affections and my will—my whole sense of who I am—are governed by the grace and mercy of God. Christian contentment repeats the basic rules of all Christian living: that we are not our own but belong to God (1 Corinthians 6:19, 20); that the only way in which we may find ourselves is giving up our own futile attempts to be in charge of our own selves (Matthew 10:39); that God's grace is sufficient, and therefore God's grace is the only route to a sense of sufficiency (2 Corinthians 12:9).

Contentment is not mastering circumstances but faith in God. But what is it that faith trusts? First, faith trusts in the providence of God (Matthew 6:25–34). God's providence is God's ordering of our lives and of the whole creation to glory. The God of providence is the God who so brings his purposes to bear on our lives that they are transformed, directed to their true goal, which is to be with God (Matthew 10:29; Romans 8:28–39). And in the end contentment derives from knowing that our lives are directed by the providential purpose of God. Trusting providence, of course, means *trusting* providence, which isn't at all the same as knowing exactly how every detail of our lives fits or does not fit into the purposes of God. Trusting providence doesn't mean we can map our lives in such a way that everything can be assigned a place on the master plan. Very often, we need to express our faith in God by saying "Nevertheless"—saying that, despite disorder and humiliation and disappointment, nevertheless God is the one who proves himself in Jesus to be the good God who wills our good and pledges himself to bring us to glory. "Though he slay me, I will hope in him" (Job 13:15).

True contentment sees this; it sees the truth of the dark side of life, faces the way we're so often disillusioned and hurt, and says, "Nevertheless, I have learned to be content."

Second, faith trusts in the sustaining presence of Jesus Christ and the power of the Holy Spirit. "I can do all things," Paul says: I can face the most adverse circumstances without being ground into the dust. How? "In him who strengthens me" (4:13 RSV). Who is this one? For Paul, it is Jesus Christ himself. We live "in" him. That is to say, our lives are what they are because he is their center, because he is the one who lives in us. Jesus Christ the living one, risen from the dead, free with the boundless liberty of God, is present to us. Through baptism we share his life, and through the Holy Spirit our lives are bound to his, so that we are, indeed, flesh of his flesh, bone of his bone. And it is because of that—because Jesus Christ is alive and through his Spirit unites us to himself—that we can endure. We have no sufficiency of ourselves; we may not rely on brains or willpower or self-control. But we may come to rest on the sufficiency of God, active in us in Christ and in the Spirit. "My grace," Paul was told, "is sufficient for you" (2 Corinthians 12:9). And so, Paul tells us, we also can come to know contentment.

So contentment is not stoic self-reliance, but the fruit of faith's deep knowledge of the providential mercy of God and the sustaining work of Christ and the Spirit. But there's another twist. All this, Paul says, is something to be *learned*: "I have learned in whatever situation I am to be content" (4:11). Contentment isn't part of our natural make-up—an innate capacity which we need to stimulate or trick into activity, perhaps, but which is basically given in our human frame. Quite the opposite, contentment flies in the face of our normal ways of going through life. It goes against the grain of all our basic instincts. It is, therefore, a hard and sometimes bitter lesson.

Learning that lesson, moreover, is not something we can do by exercising our best powers of mind and will, even our religious powers. Nor is it something we can acquire simply by the passing of years. True spiritual contentment is not a mellowing of the soul, accepting the rough with the smooth and not letting ourselves get too aggravated by our lot. Some of us may be more naturally "contented" than others, of course; some of us, no doubt, may mature into it. But over and above these natural human goings-on in our souls, Christian contentment is the Spirit's gift. It derives from the Holy Spirit who shows us the truth of the gospel of God. It is sustained by the Holy Spirit who reminds us of the reality of Jesus Christ. *Learning* contentment is thus a spiritual matter. It is not about applying our powers in a certain way; it is about becoming a new person, a person caught up by God's Spirit, re-created, converted. In talking about contentment, therefore, Paul is not just talking of one of life's lessons picked up along the way. He is talking about one of the fruits of regeneration, of being made anew.

What does this mean in practical terms? First and foremost, it means that to learn contentment we need to begin somewhere other than ourselves. We need to begin, not with ourselves, our situation and distresses, but with the gospel—that amazing announcement that God is God for us and with us. We need to begin with what the gospel tells us of Christ who is alive, and of the Spirit who binds us to Christ. We need to begin there because if we don't, we'll more than likely find ourselves defeated in our search for contentment. And beginning with the gospel, with Christ and the Spirit, we need to pray. We need, that is, to cry to God in our discontent, knowing that we can do nothing of ourselves.

Perhaps more than anything else, we need to pray that we might *see*. Paul learned contentment because through faith he saw the reality of God. He saw that his life as an apostle was not a shot in the dark, not chaos and suffering and defeat, but something undergirded and preserved by God. Because he saw that—because he knew and trusted that reality more than anything else—he learned sufficiency. So it is with us: We are to pray that we may learn how to see ourselves aright, how to grasp the simple truth which eludes us nearly all the time, that God is good, that Jesus Christ is alive for us, that his Spirit lives in us to transfigure our lives, that we will be brought to fulfillment in him.

There is, of course, no fast track to contentment. Many of us, looking at our record in this matter, would see little progress and a good deal of backsliding. Most obviously, this is because in our perversity we don't want to see God or know how to look for him. We do not sustain our gaze. Often we prefer our discontent, and it becomes a badge of honor, a way of manipulating others into sympathy or respect, or a way of making sure we're left alone. But for Christians now, at least in the West, there also are real cultural blockages to contentment. We find ourselves in a culture which by and large thinks contentment is worthless. A culture organized around acquisition cannot be the seedbed of contentment, because it thrives on dissatisfaction, on wanting something which is *more*, or just *other*, than we have now. Most of us find ourselves trapped in a way of life which inflames beyond all proportion our appetite for what is new. And the price is restlessness or a sense of being permanently dissatisfied with whatever we have or are.

Part of the task of God's people is to demonstrate the quiet, happy dignity of spiritual contentment. "Now there is great gain in godliness with contentment" (1 Timothy 6:6). In this respect, there is a particular witness to be borne in demonstrating contentment in the face of want. One of the ways in which Christian people may point to the healing effect of the gospel is by showing how to be abased, how to face disillusionment and lack of fulfillment. No one gets through life unscathed; everyone has to abandon some hope for some fulfillment which they might reasonably expect but which never comes. We look for fulfillment in our work, but often it eludes us; we long for friendship, or good health, or a sense of our own worthiness in the eyes of others, but it slips from our grasp. Christians aren't called to ignore these disappointments; contentment isn't complacency. Still less are we called to silence our anguish at them, as if the truth could be denied. But we're called to see want and disappointment differently, to see them in the light of God's ordering of our lives and in the light of the truth of the gospel. God is, and God is gracious.

Such is the situation in which we find ourselves. And here the gospel instructs us to ask God to frame our lives in such a way that we may see the truth and, humbly and gently, live in its reality.

And so we pray:

> *Teach us, O Father, in whatsoever state we are, therewith to be content, that we may know both how to be abased and how to abound; that in prosperity we may bless thee who givest us richly all things to enjoy, and in adversity may not suffer our faith in thy love to fail; through Jesus Christ our Lord. Amen.*

CHAPTER 25

DO NOT BE ANXIOUS

Matthew 6:25–34

Therefore I tell you, do not be anxious about your life, what you will eat or what you will drink, nor about your body, what you will put on. Is not life more than food, and the body more than clothing? Look at the birds of the air: they neither sow nor reap nor gather into barns, and yet your heavenly Father feeds them. Are you not of more value than they? And which of you by being anxious can add a single hour to his span of life? And why are you anxious about clothing? Consider the lilies of the field, how they grow: they neither toil nor spin, yet I tell you, even Solomon in all his glory was not arrayed like one of these. But if God so clothes the grass of the field, which today is alive and tomorrow is thrown into the oven, will he not much more clothe you, O you of little faith? Therefore do not be anxious, saying, 'What shall we eat?' or 'What shall we drink?' or 'What shall we wear?' For the Gentiles seek after all these things, and your heavenly Father knows that you need them all. But seek first the kingdom of God and his righteousness, and all these things will be added to you.

Therefore do not be anxious about tomorrow, for tomorrow will be anxious for itself. Sufficient for the day is its own trouble.

Matthew 6:25–34

Honesty surely compels us to begin by saying that as we hear this passage from the Sermon on the Mount, we find it simply absurd. How can this be considered a remotely serious recommendation about how we're to conduct ourselves? Are we not to take care of ourselves? Are we not to take responsibility for our lives? Surely, we want to say to this teacher, no sound and solid economy, and no good order of human society and individual life, can be rooted in this dangerous injunction: "Do not be anxious." And so, shaking our heads, we may walk away dismayed.

Of course, good pious Christians that we are, we may be tempted to suppress our feelings of dismay—to think that it's rather unworthy of us to react negatively to the good Lord's teaching. Perhaps what we ought to do is to try and knock off some of its rough edges, so that it becomes a bit less offensive. Maybe Jesus is just indulging in hyperbole, to keep us from over-investing in material things and letting them preoccupy us to the point of worry.

For my part, however, it seems more honest and in the end much more fruitful to face up to the offense of Jesus' saying. Indeed, it's only when we do that—when we look head-on at the fact that this material makes us want to just turn away—that we actually run up against what's really basic to Jesus' teaching here. Only when we realize how disturbing it is to our conventional ways of thinking about reality can we see that what is set before us is nothing short of the sheer miracle of God and God's kingdom. For it's this miracle, and the upheaval which this miracle generates in our day-to-day life, which Jesus in the Sermon on the Mount sets before us. And, as always in trying to let Jesus' teaching sink into our minds and spirits, we first have to feel that it's a rock of offense, a stone over which we stumble and fall. Only then can we know that what we hear is a word of grace and mercy.

"Do not be anxious," Jesus tells us. What's the anxiety in mind here? The anxiety which Jesus here exposes to the light of his judgment has two elements: It's a state of the soul, and it's a form of activity.

The anxiety of which the gospel speaks here is more than simply feeling worried; it's more than the passing apprehension which all of us feel about going to the dentist or facing a difficult interview. Those kinds of apprehensions are a matter of fear; we know what troubles us, and with the right sort of determined effort to screw up our courage, we resolve to face them. But anxiety is a sickness. Anxiety is that sickness of the soul in which what might happen to us fills us with dread. When we're anxious, our future as a whole, the possibilities which stretch out ahead of us, becomes a matter not of hope but of terror.

Anxiety is a terrifying shadow of our uniquely human capacity to hope. When we hope, we project ourselves into the future, imagining what it may be and stretching out toward it with longing. But when we're anxious, our imaginations busy themselves with images of the threats which the future has in store for us. We fill in the gap between now and the future with all sorts of disturbing possibilities, and they eat us up. Anxiety makes us feel that the world has somehow slipped through our fingers and that we have no control over our own destiny.

It's this fear which drives anxiety into activity. Fear properly issues in resolution and courage; anxiety produces a sort of helpless, unfocused busyness. Courage is a gathering of myself and my resources so that I can face what makes me afraid with a kind of single-minded clarity of purpose. Courage, that is, clarifies and concentrates the soul. But anxiety does the opposite; it dissipates our energies. Above all, it makes us think that we can survive only if we take charge. We have to be omni-competent if we are to shed our anxieties, and so we climb onto the merciless treadmill of working harder and harder, somehow to keep everything together. Above all, anxiety is bound up with our desperate need for *security*—the need to know that we will be OK, that we will survive intact, that at the end of the day we will *be*.

This sickness of the soul is, of course, not only a private grief. It takes cultural and political form, too: Societies and institutions can be anxious in their way, driven by a need for reassurance in the face of the uncertainties of the future. Institutional rigidity, the demarcation of the world into friends and enemies, competitiveness, and the elaboration of forms of social control, all express the same deep-seated worry that we may not have a future unless we make one for ourselves. And to those terrors, too, as well as to our personal nightmares, Jesus says: "Do not be anxious."

How on earth can he say that? How on earth can he expect us to take him seriously? To answer these questions, we need to listen very carefully to what's being said to us here in the gospel. Jesus isn't reinforcing some bit of conventional human wisdom. He's not, as it were, coming into the midst of the human situation and lending the weight of his authority to a truism which has been known all down the ages—that fussing and fretting damages the equilibrium of human life, that anxiety distracts and hurts us. No: He is telling us, his hearers, that what rules out anxiety is the sheer fact of himself. He himself, Jesus Christ, the presence of God's kingdom, the rule of God in creation—that's what finally shows the truth of our anxiety. In him, it's finally shown to be the sickness which it is.

What is, then, the anxiety from which Jesus seeks to detach us? Very simply, it's our failure to grasp and live out of the significance of Jesus Christ. Anxiety is our failure—sometimes from fear, sometimes from pride—to allow that, in and as the man

Jesus, God rules all things in heaven and earth, and therefore that our lives are in God's good hands. When Jesus summons us from anxiety, he injects into the world of our responsibilities something utterly new, utterly different. He breaks the world of anxiety apart by saying that this world—the world of daily life and care, the world of work and responsibility—isn't a world in which we and we alone have to bear the burden of ensuring that we survive. This world is the place of God's kingdom; here, God's rule in Jesus Christ is the great new factor.

Because this is true, Jesus tells us, we may come to learn that daily life is not a place where we're devoured by the need to shore ourselves up against disaster. Daily life is the place where we encounter God as the one whom he calls our "heavenly Father." Who is this Father? He's the one who knows our needs, because we are not hidden from him; and he's the one who provides for our needs, because he loves what he has made in all its fragility and impermanence—because he desires that we should flourish. And if God is like that—if God isn't a threat hanging over us but the astonishing Father of lavish grace—then anxiety is a kind of illusion: It doesn't match up to what reality is truly like.

What does match up to reality, Jesus tells us, is faith. Faith sees the truth about God and God's merciful, gracious kingdom which is embodied for us in Jesus Christ. Faith is not just some crazy hope against evidence (indeed, when it becomes that it is itself a kind of sickness). Quite the opposite: Faith is that deeply healthy state of the soul in which we let God be God. It's that free, unhesitating, joyful assent to the one in the midst of whose kingdom we stand secure.

This contrast between anxiety and faith is the force of the little comparison with the birds of the air and the lilies of the field. The non-human creation offers a picture of immediate, unself-conscious, unreflective trust. It's the antithesis of fretful anxiety, the opposite of all those efforts devoted to filling in the gap between now and the future. And so it offers us a parable of faith. Not to heed that parable, Jesus tells his hearers, is to act like what he calls "the nations" or "the Gentiles." Anxiety properly speaking is only fitting for those who think of themselves as outside the circle of God's covenant, beyond the edges of the promises of God and the kingdom of his Son. For the disciples of Jesus to be anxious is for them to act as if, somehow, God's covenant were not true; as if his kingdom were not among us; as if we may not trust the word of grace which is spoken in Jesus.

What instruction may we take from this passage for ourselves? I don't think we'll get too far in making sense of what's said to us here unless we let ourselves be pulled up short by its revolutionary force. What's identified here is not an occasional or partial disease which may or may not afflict human life; what's identified is a whole world of human living and acting. Anxiety is not a private disorder of the personality which some of us have to struggle with, but an entire way of being human in the world. And so the call that we shouldn't be anxious isn't an invitation to personal religious therapy. It's a call to take very seriously the great imperative of the gospel: "seek first the kingdom of God" (6:33). What does it mean to seek God's kingdom?

When Jesus talks of seeking God's kingdom, he isn't telling us that the kingdom is some hidden reality which we have to struggle to lay bare. God's kingdom doesn't lie at the end of some great quest, and seeking it isn't to be an occasion for spiritual athleticism. To seek God's kingdom is simply to acknowledge that it is already among us, supremely potent and effective in the ministry of the man Jesus. To seek God's kingdom thus means in public and in private, politically and domestically, to order our affections in such a way that God in Christ is the supreme reality. It means to govern our thinking and acting by the sheer truth that Jesus Christ is the one in whom God renews the face of the earth; it means to acknowledge that all other ways of thinking and acting fail, because they don't read the world as it truly is: the place of God's kingly rule. To "seek" that rule is, we might say, to strive after and hasten toward God's rule as the most real reality and truest truth that may be found.

Such is the imperative. Jesus doesn't spell out in detail what that imperative will involve for each of us. We're left to work out what it means for our possessions and our insurance policies. But, as always in the gospel, the imperative isn't the last word. The last word is grace. God's grace is nothing other than the name of Jesus Christ, for it's in him that our anxieties are finally set aside as utterly pointless. We must not be anxious because we need not be anxious. Our present experience of life may be very dark, undoubtedly. We may face fearful prospects. But even at its most burdensome, our lives now are not perilously poised over some great chasm into which we may fall at any time. No, our lives are hidden with Christ in God. And our future isn't some dark possibility lying over the horizon waiting to devour us. No, it's the place where we will encounter the glory of God in the face of Jesus Christ. That's why we're told that all things will be added to us.

Let me end with some words of a Christian martyr who discovered even in death the freedom from anxiety which is here commended to us:

> Jesus does not tell us what we ought to do but cannot; he tells us what God has given us and promises still to give. If Christ has been given us, if we are called to his discipleship, we are given all things. ... He will see to it that they are added unto us. If we follow Jesus and look only unto his righteousness, we are in his hands and under the protection of him and his Father. And if we are in communion with the Father, nothing can harm us. We shall always be assured that he will feed his children and

will not suffer them to hunger. God will help us in the hour of need, and he knows our needs.[1]

1. Dietrich Bonhoeffer, *The Cost of Discipleship* (London: SCM Press, 2001), 125.

CHAPTER 26

THE DAY OF GOD

2 Peter 3:8–14

But do not overlook this one fact, beloved, that with the Lord one day is as a thousand years, and a thousand years as one day. The Lord is not slow to fulfill his promise as some count slowness, but is patient toward you, not wishing that any should perish, but that all should reach repentance. But the day of the Lord will come like a thief, and then the heavens will pass away with a roar, and the heavenly bodies will be burned up and dissolved, and the earth and the works that are done on it will be exposed.

Since all these things are thus to be dissolved, what sort of people ought you to be in lives of holiness and godliness, waiting for and hastening the coming of the day of God, because of which the heavens will be set on fire and dissolved, and the heavenly bodies will melt as they burn! But according to his promise we are waiting for new heavens and a new earth in which righteousness dwells.

Therefore, beloved, since you are waiting for these, be diligent to be found by him without spot or blemish, and at peace.

2 Peter 3:8–14

THERE IS, OR AT LEAST THERE OUGHT TO BE, a certain *tension* in the Church's celebration of Advent. Properly celebrated, Advent ought to lay upon us the need for focus, for concentration in the life of Christian discipleship. Being an Advent Christian, a member of the community of Advent, involves being jolted into a heightened sense of the reality of our situation before God, a kind of simplification in which what's important and what's peripheral becomes plain to us. Now, of all times, we are to learn what does or doesn't matter. What generates this Advent purging of our spirits is the stark and devastatingly simple reminder that the day of God is at hand. We are, now, in the last times; we stand at the close of the ages.

Second Peter lays the point before us with some of the stock-in-trade pictures of the end times: "the day of the Lord will come like a thief, and then the heavens will pass away with a roar, and the heavenly bodies will be burned up and dissolved, and the earth and the works that are done on it will be exposed" (3:10). It's a picture of *dissolution*: What we take to be the firm structures of the world—the fabric of natural reality, the order of time and space and matter, the great solid works of human life and culture—all this, like some great city in an earthquake, will fall into ruin, lose its solidity and its firmness and be consumed. The real point, however, is not just this unimaginable cosmic disaster; that's only a symptom. The reality to which it all points is *God in his coming*. The end of nature and history, the meltdown of all that exists, is in the end only a sign—a sign of the day of the Lord, the day of God. And that day, 2 Peter tells us, is the day of judgment. It is the day of truth, the day on which God will finally and authoritatively declare the truth of human life, and finally and authoritatively establish his rule over all things. The day of God is the day on which God's truth, God's order, God's righteousness are vindicated and acknowledged to be utterly real.

Now, making sense of all this requires a remarkable leap of mind and spirit for us. At best, it all sounds pretty implausible; at worst, it sounds like the apocalyptic imagination run riot, offending good taste and sound reason alike. But we need to ask why it seems so implausible, even offensive, to us. What is it that makes us balk at this point? In the end it's something spiritual; something in us resists. What we resist, sometimes desperately, is the idea that human life and human history might be broken off, blown apart, once and for all interrupted and dissolved. We build our whole lives around the assumption that everything will carry on pretty much as it is; that it will be meaningful to have a career, marry and raise children, build a culture, write a book, look to tranquility in retirement. We can't seem to work without the steady assumption that our lives and times stretch out in front of us and that we will work and hope, reaching out into future time. Of course, in one sense, we're quite right to do so. We have to carry on, we have to build, we have to make a future for ourselves. But the crucial point is this: We aren't to do so in a way which excludes the coming of God and of God's judgment. In making our lives, in building our future, we must leave ourselves open to the day of God. If we don't—if we build lives and institutions in such a way that the coming day of God has been forgotten—then we've not even begun to understand what the gospel requires of us.

It is against all this that Advent is four weeks of solid protest. Advent lodges in the middle of the life of the Church a contradiction of the whole process in which human life and culture and politics and even religion can become one busy evasion of God. Advent tells us that the truly wise person is not the person who builds a life of such solidity and firmness that nothing can shake it. No, the truly wise person is one who lives and travels light, who doesn't invest too deeply, who is open to judgment. Advent tells us that communities which build their political lives around an idea of invulnerability, which assume that the earth and the works on it will remain forever, are in the end idolatrous. Advent tells us that ways of religious belief which like to think that everything about God can be fixed with routines and habits and order are not ways of discipleship, but ways of resisting God's claim upon us. For these things also are to be dissolved, burned up, and brought to nothing.

Having heard the Advent protest, having recognized that all things are to be dissolved, what ought we to *do*, what sort of people ought we to be? Very simply, 2 Peter indicates that we are to live "lives of holiness and godliness, waiting for and hastening the coming day of God" (3:11–12). Notice, most of all, that we are to *do* something. The coming day of God, the judgment and dissolution of all things, is not meant to paralyze us, to freeze us into immobility like rabbits caught in the light. Rather, it's a command, an imperative; it urges us to act *now*. And it urges us to action which is fitting for what's coming—to live our lives now, in this Advent in-between, in such a way that we anticipate and live for the great future of God. Our life now is to be a foretaste of what it will mean to live in the great future of the day of God. We are to be godly, to fashion our lives after the pattern of God himself, set out supremely in the way of Jesus Christ. We are to be holy, to echo the character of the God who has set us apart for his own purposes and called us to be his people. Above all, we are to wait, to hasten toward, to earnestly desire and work toward God's coming—to fix our hope and affections and wills, to be undistracted in making that coming our focus and goal and fulfillment (3:12–14). And in so doing, in being people who are and do these things, we will anticipate the new heavens and the new earth, "in which righteousness dwells" (3:13).

Put very simply, Advent calls us to live now in anticipation of the new world of God.

But how do we do this? How do we live in anticipation? Two things are of paramount importance. First, we are to wait for the coming of God. Very often in the New Testament, the real distinctiveness of the people of God is that they await his coming. While others sleep or carouse or get bogged down in all the world's entanglements, God's people are alert and on the watch (1 Thessalonians 5:2–4). They will not be caught out by the Lord's coming, because they have made a firm decision and have kept at their post and have not ceased to watch for the coming of God (see Matthew 25:1–13). We likewise are to be the kind of people who do not slumber in the face of God's coming. There are a million reasons for getting distracted, of course: career, culture, the cares of the world, our own doubts, the scorn or polite disregard of others, the seeming absence of the God who has promised so much. But the command stands: wait; watch. We're not commanded to build buildings and write books and create cultures, though we may do these things, too; but we are commanded to hold ourselves ready, to be zealous to be found waiting by him at his coming.

Second, as those who wait we're also to be those who try to live with the right kind of attachments to the world. Once the first Christian communities figured out that the coming day of God was not just around the corner and had to dig themselves in for the long haul, they had to work out a way of living in the world which meant both accepting the necessity of families and jobs and possessions and communities and also trying to steer clear of their entanglements, making sure that those necessary things didn't lull them to sleep. Things are no different for us. We can't abandon any attempt to build a life and just sit and wait (2 Thessalonians 3:6–13), but we can learn the wisdom of dispossession (so 1 Corinthians 9). We can learn that what we have and build is for now but not forever, and so dispossess ourselves of all those things—often those good things—which rob us of God. That is at least one of the things meant by putting away the works of darkness and putting on the armor of light (Romans 13:12).

Lastly, if all this sounds strange, no one should be too surprised. The world is out of joint, and so are we. Our appetites, our affections, don't run straight; they attach themselves to the wrong things, or attach themselves to the right things in the wrong ways. And so Advent invites us to repentance. But more than anything, it invites us to prayer. And that prayer begins: "Almighty God, give us grace." Advent discipline, Advent wisdom, turning to the coming of God, is God's own gift. We don't know how to wait, how to hasten, how to be godly and holy; these things are in the hands of God. But so are we. And so now, in the time of this mortal life, we may be taught by the Spirit of God how to trust his promise and wait for the new heavens and the new earth in which righteousness dwells. Amen.

Scripture Index

Old Testament

New Testament

Sermon Delivery Index

Sermons (here given with their titles in this work) were originally delivered on the following occasions:

Chapter 1—"The Lie of Self-Sufficiency"
Christ Church Cathedral, Oxford; 1 April 1999

Chapter 2—"The Great Contrast"
Brentwood United Reformed Church, Essex; 1 July 2000

Chapter 3—"Believe in the Lord Jesus"
Christ Church Cathedral, Oxford; Date unknown

Chapter 4—"Dead to Sin"
Christ Church Cathedral, Oxford; 27 June 1999

Chapter 5—"He Who Comforts"
Christ Church Cathedral, Oxford; 8 December 2002

Chapter 6—"Hearing the Passion"
Christ Church Cathedral, Oxford; 23 March 1997

Chapter 7—"Sin Shattered within its Stronghold"
Christ Church Cathedral, Oxford; 12 April 2001

Chapter 8—"Lifted High in Humiliation"
Christ Church Cathedral, Oxford; 13 April 2001

Chapter 9—"Take this Holy Sacrament"
Christ Church Cathedral, Oxford; 14 April 2001

Chapter 10—"The Triumph of Divine Resolve"
Christ Church Cathedral, Oxford; 15 April 2001

Chapter 11—"Listen to Him"
St. Thomas of Canterbury, Goring-on-Thames; 5 March 2000

Chapter 12—"Praising God"
The Chapel of the Cross, Dallas, Texas; 27 September 2002

Chapter 13—"Belonging to God"
The Chapel of the Cross, Dallas, Texas; 28 September 2002

Chapter 14—"Obeying God"
The Chapel of the Cross, Dallas, Texas; 29 September 2002

Chapter 15—"The Hearing Church"
Hertford College, Oxford; 25 May 2003

Chapter 16—"God's Sustaining Presence"
King's College Chapel, Aberdeen, Scotland; 6 November 2005

Chapter 17—"The Call to Remembrance"
Wycliffe Hall, Oxford; 3 December 1997

Chapter 18—"The Nature of Faith"
Christ Church Cathedral, Oxford; 19 March 2000

Chapter 19—"The Way of Holiness"
Christ Church Cathedral, Oxford; 31 October 1999

Chapter 20—"Yes in Christ"
Christ Church Cathedral, Oxford; 27 September 1997

Chapter 21—"The Heart of Perseverance"
Christ Church Cathedral, Oxford; 1 May 2003

Chapter 22—"Endurance"
Christ Church Cathedral, Oxford; 8 October 2000

Chapter 23—"Waiting Patiently"
Christ Church Cathedral, Oxford; 27 July 2003

Chapter 24—"Christian Contentment"
Christ Church Cathedral, Oxford; 20 February 2000

Chapter 25—"Do Not Be Anxious"
Christ Church Cathedral, Oxford; 15 February 1998

Chapter 26—"The Day of God"
Christ Church Cathedral, Oxford; 5 December 1999